Babble On to Babylon

blem vide

AF008285

PretendGeniusPress
London, New York, San Francisco, Seattle, Washington D.C.

In rhyme before reason.

The obligatory legal disclaimer:
All Rights (and Wrongs) Reserved ©2004 by Adam
www.blemvide.com
Except for brief passages quoted in space, radio or television review, no part of this funny little book may be reproduced or transmitted in any form or by any means, graphic, electronic, mnemonic, psychic or mechanical, including photocopying, recording, or by any information storage retrieval system, without permission in writing from the publisher. We'll get you.

A few pages of this stuff appeared at writeThis.com.
(please mail that check to my pocket)

PretendGeniusPress
www.pretendgenius.com
ISBN: 0-9747261-8-4

Printed in the United States of America!

Contents

I *Glasgow Gas Glow Glass Gallery*

Art Without Instructions   *9*
My Life Could Be Falling Apart   *12*
Mossomog   *15*
Babylon Pose   *21*
Belly Dancing   *23*
Golden Pennies From Lady Luck   *33*
Serrapine Jungle   *35*
Animajade   *37*
Dejection Specialists   *41*
Noetry Extempore   *43*
Tiny Futures (Atomic Center)   *46*

II *Serve the Creative Impulse, Idiots*

I'm Like, So Full of Shiite   *57*
Serve the Creative Impulse, Idiots   *58*
Back to Abacus   *63*
Go Spies Go   *64*
August Step Dehydrate Tape   *69*
Egyptian Reverb   *81*
A Peruvian Love Song   *83*
Protecting Intellectual Property by Giving It Away   *85*
Imitation of A Newspaper Column   *89*
I'm Dropping My Balloon   *92*
Zapruder Clap Track   *93*

III *Dig Big Baggy Grotto Mob Mottos*

For Good Golly Miss Molly's Poetry Class   *97*
Egoless Shtick   *98*
Self Interview   *99*
Rigva Raga Loop   *105*
Dig Big Baggy Grotto Mob Mottos   *106*
Eek Out A Genius   *109*
Ego Coughing   *111*
Opportunities Fly By   *117*
Keep Hope Alive   *120*
Motors   *122*
Ulahan the Latuganist   *124*

IV *Blem Vide is a Problem Provider*

Brief Results Prolonged   *129*
Love Machine in Graffiti   *132*
Losing Your Insignificance Back   *134*
Tributaries   *138*
Roll on Maharishi   *140*
I Am Chair   *143*
The Art of Self-Defeat   *145*
Missing Car Keys Indeed   *146*
Basura Monologue   *147*
Valley of Broken Language   *148*
Soviet Museum of Fine Arts   *151*

Biographical Timeline   *163*

I / Glasgow Gas Glow Glass Gallery

Employed to the void & verily overjoyed.

Art Without Instructions (an art disclaimer)

Not all art is well thought-out, I think

art is a survivor of love thrown in the trash
to avoid explaining what 'sunshine echo' means

art is your trash
trash is a round table
do not forget that, folks

art isn't trash
and trash is a round table
art is a round table

a round table is a
psychological symbol of trash
art is a recycled telephone book

"how is art a recycled telephone book? are you being sarcastic?"

art is 2 parts iodine & 3 parts warm urine

"are you putting me on? is this automatic free-association?"

have you noticed the CIA in association?

*"well, yes, now that you mention it,
I do see the CIA in association"*

fool,
art is the ASS
in association
not the CIA

okay?

art may be trash
but trash isn't necessarily art

art is perfectly casual
smooth as astro glide
universe & space-time
is causal not casual

art laughs at me sounding smart
as if by accident (and not fraud)

again, art is an accident

art can be
textually appalling
or art can come calling
your name in divorce court

art can be the west nile virus, orange alerts,
security checks, snipers, honest comets,
four quartets, fascist ashes, or a modest
recycle bin laden caveman
boo!

art could be a gay pirate dressed up
as a ditzy blonde in g-string
and you'd have no control over it
get over it

art can be the result
of years effort
or a gimmicky toss-off

or art can come from
feeling sick
and banging on keys

art is perfectly casual
just as usual
even if you spell it
against power

In art as in life — be just.
But if you cannot be just — be arbitrary.

Just relax
act casual

yes, art is
perfectly agile

art is a smashed atom
art is naturally irrational

art is smooth, not obvious
or very obvious
perfectly casual
just as usual

by the way,
if you're comfortable
you're wrong

art spies on you

you are being watched
and described
not always in a flattering way

smile if you need instructions

(and if you're smiling now, you owe me lunch)

My Life Could Be Falling Apart

my life could be falling apart
and you wouldn't know about it
I could be unemployed
with a wife and two kids
and you wouldn't know

I could be dying of sunshine
stroking a laugh catheter
that tingles my prostate
and you won't be kept up to date
on my prognosis

I might act fabulously gay on Sundays
just to spite my Bushite neighbors
I might perform small clitoral favors
for drive-thru lesbian muff dives
and you won't know if blem is a vide
or a five-time karaoke jive

I have a state job as file clerk for crissakes

or maybe I volunteer free legal services
to welfare mothers and gimp poets
who bitch and moan about people
who don't know the difference
between the former and the latter
and your attention span doesn't matter

who are you again?

I might have toy guns
aimed at my mailbox
I could be reading fire
to wild cactus juice
cooked under a Joshua tree
and I still can't tell you about
my 3 fastest-fading loves

aahh the guilt grows in my enemy's trees

I eat jellybread with a secret sophist topping
I drink Glitterhouse wine to project my progression
of neglected vanity projects I subjectively object to

but you aren't in the loop, are you?

meanwhile
the part of yourself you left
behind your eyelids
as you read over this
is brewing over
an Asian tea bag synapse
dub relapse spit in the soul hole
dropped in the fishbowl
casually subliminal

communicating information is out of service
please use the handrail to your left
to guide you back to your piecemeal
bit by bit torrent forming an orange
doorhinge on the cornerstone's edge
I hedge on in eight-fifths precisely
 -give or take a cinched inch of my eyebrow

go measure for yourself, I ain't telling you about it

I'm mopping up the floor
of kitchen liquor stores
with underscores
of you fuckers

my life could be a morality play
at an old folks home
in shiny shiny Utah
when the Mormons come home

I could be born from a long line
of hygiene products
and you'd never know about it

I might be a smother of invention
who dabbles in ballet bullets
shot from gut rot funk macramé
that I can't say enough about
and I won't be telling you about it

why should I?

I could have vitamins pumped into
my limousine and you wouldn't
smell the vitamin C breeze

what have you done for me lately?

Mossomog

Detroit locusts can have my melancholy life.
I am so completely sick of this isn't serious.
But I insist on a rogue symmetry in my files.
When the sun shines courageously on your face,
so begins Gershwin. I can't bust a nut like that,
but I still feel dignified. Your gaffed screen presence
blots out siamese chemistry and I feel guilty about
alamo wheels singing over grapevines and ivy tribes
of motion memory in the poorer districts of our city.
I also can't remember if this was a question?

I remember motion signs moving millennium
celebrations from the front page of *Harper's Bazaar*
to the bizarre pages in *Melting Hands Honor Blind Spots*.
I remember a million mad databases dividing into
diamond bamboo shoots. If you are also taking an
MAIO inhibitor, you might feel a critical groove
to move & joy cruise solo. My apologies.

Enjoy marbled love found in an electrical ditch- two
dollars short of retiring to a media counterspin post,
exposing nerve endings to a frayed tooth spat out in
true blue sauna rave style, dig it. That was an attitude
joke. But see how it made a coffee cup go yuppie.
Happy is a byword pasta dish covered with all
eight identical party favors of casual bliss,
on Catalonian shag carpet.

I hid myself from my errant policies in
Kosovo, excuse me, Marilyn Monroe.
I had a bad few mornings in a row.
As opposed to a row of too few bad days.

Seems I've displaced the light of Bare Ass cinema.

Sweeten the hostage gloves. Atomic Gene tourists
dodge insults at a dutch meeting of hand grenades with
careful church water. Is it cool we relax now? I figured
out five thousand new worlds of order upon a spiritual
retreat's glow, in light of the holy digits of Santa Cruz.
It's never enough to truly convince me that nothing is
wrong. Spending my minutes up the parochial slopes of
an abandoned Mossomog.

Never sit in awe of a product or a bit of gypsy advice
stealing your hum drive theatre push. That ring on your
finger is a decoder symbol of how far we go from early
id (our id) to becoming personal yawn pinnacles at the
sight of urban pimping, arson fires. Not every house is
a limousine, but not every house can speak cottage.

In the background of not every scene scheduled to
be filmed soon, we see several mechanical postcards
delivering themselves back to curious senders. She,
being one, replies *"my life is your main curiosity. My throne
is taking care of our gifted appearance with the drinking of boiled
tea from leaves dating back to irreverent Mayan fringe tribes."*

The white men laughed like hyenas while praying for
extra poison out of sunshine and acid rain. An adaptive
body diet is plumbed into my body under Cherry trees.

Come watch verbal communication in arc orbits
rapid-dry intoxicant ebbs with me. I'm studying
Sloganistics As Gimmicks to throw future goop on
my alien ticklers. Am I sorry for not making-up
detective stories or for being an assassin-free brother?
Hey, a lot of armies are envious of my penis.
What can I say? Wait, I made that up?
You must be sorry I don't feel very personal?

General plans for basic vox pop oppression call for mood looters and arboretum loiterers to enter stage left via flea markets to work tire booths and fruit stands. This was my back porch before I stole it from the cops.

I hear copper wire calculating an abortion of my legal rights as I come damn close to a month of my secret codex moaning. It feels damn good. But I can't afford to retain a lawyer. My dubious situation, of course, involves a sweet crucifix icon style of life I used in my early youth trials, just the other day. I behaved sluggishly in court. At age 24 I started a passive but constant campaign against the soul-impaired shock of recognition planet Assoul. Sheeple. Bahhhh.

Hey Mr DJ, how's that radio song go? Do you still roll your own cigarettes down uninspired alleyways? Am I still sold out? Am I allowed to revisit the lame crème de menthe town? Why don't I like Beer?

If I had the resources to pull together a slingshot aim at a thumbprint lightening shower, it would be a noble magnetic theme of antipode cassette reel recordings of meteor glints and super optical grease. I cannot open a net of collective hands closed. You don't remember the tightrope act drunk on black feet balancing a gravity poem above an average number?

Whip steady tremolo tones with heavy trumpet breathing translate into warm food in a bedroom of bellies without wall glitches, pitching a floating rumor ceiling jive, chasing a rattling civic cage in the doorjamb phobia. No, you don't have to rely on those ideas, in fact I wouldn't. Time for a mental break - but only if you don't love yourself, says King Wen.

If a way out of an international spy ring begins as a
secondary route to expression for Spanish heritage,
an architectural milieu will erupt a million stonecutter
anti-library jabs. So to protect our postures we must
study our own effects in mirrors. Vanity is nothing to
fear, unless you are intimidated by beauty. Then the
only consequence you might endure is a worn-out
corner of knowledge to wield in defense of shadow
hobbies. So be careful.

What you know may be rotten fruit or poison bread,
better digested with an empty mind full of heaven?
Yes, and either chore is a third door to take a little
less seriously. Knowledge is too expensive.

Okay, folks, if you're still curious about mystical crap:
your most drunken epiphanies always stir up an acre
of that misguided urban coincidence expansion rap.
I can't keep track of your secret knocks & handshakes.
You're just a silly little notion in a big bad world of
unlimited jokes, and you back-up sly on the defense to
tell me about how libelous slander cuts both ways. But I
never hear you. Not because I'm financially sound,
which sounds good, but because I'm a mischievous
character with clean clothes and bad haircuts.
No, actually I'm a Jesuit horse flogger.

A specific object from a velvet bag is chosen by our
fearless Leader last before choosing to cast suspicions
into the aquarium of vague details. What the hell, the
cursive voices? God's movies fade into daily nexus
details quickly forgotten to make room in the mind
for turbo Kama Sutra in rhyme ad nausea.

Plenty plenum, a plethora of pablum.
That's my platitude for ya.

Other examples: 1st trick object selected from a bag mocks a potentially dangerous safety pin casually dropped to the floor in a motel room. Next, a vote object is interwoven along a chosen path of caring for sick people. It's good work, an ego healer should commend you.

I'll show you how quick an idea can be blown into dramatic dregs. Well, I'd show you but I've already moved on to that unnamable bliss of the opposite. Have you ever wondered what the opposite of an idea being blown into dramatic dregs is?

A symbolic death of a plot not fleshed out for years to come to compensate for ten-minute stories swept under rugs in front of filing cabinets with personality tonality woodwork falling asleep at the gates of high paradise before the door swings open and my name becomes a grain of sand. This is improv comedy as far as I'm concerned, and I'm borrowing your money to pay my bills. That line always kills the mood of an audience.

I'd love to be able to thread 120,600 ideas into four chapters of my Unruly Disposition Directive, but my disposition changes daily and I haven't decided what I want a particular character's life to represent. I will be represented as a character. I'm new at this. Anyway, in order for a character's life to represent a meaningful position, I'd have to devise a system of rules and footnotes on their idiosyncratic natures, which would take up a lot of my precious time.

Then I'd have to think about what exactly happens every second of a characters life, and whether my documentation is flexible enough to both entertain and twist the gaunt facts.

Lies must be fat enough to nourish themselves
without tapping into the secret reserve of truth.

Poor truth, herded into private queues by radical
Quakers, then divvied up in 3 even halves.
Two halves will polarize any possibility of an even
defeat of a readers ego. One half will imply a rainfall
echo, which will divert your attention away from the
scene of the crime.

Candy anyone?

Besides, I have no clue as to what I'm talking about.
I'm just a-pratting along on a comical beat, two shakes
in Israel and one long narrow pain in my heart.

An imaginary grain tower in ancient Babylon collapses
like a lung from hysterical laughter when it finds out
I referenced it in a project I was working on. And I
further implied that the Tower was constructed only
to collapse anyway, be it from something I thought
thousands of years later or from it's own histrionic
gambling debts, but probably from my lazy habits.

I manufacture my own guilt, and gamble with it.

Babylon Pose

Lost my Baby
To a culture's gravy
Lost my Baby
to the eye spice
mile-high gravity
All-American graffiti

Lost my Baby
to a youth bomb
Lost my Baby
to a sausage crawl
Ah, she's yapping out loud
about the thrills and the perks
of her flirts with money affairs
while her purse is full of gummy bears

she sings London, she sings France
she sings in Canada's underpants
she loves to dance naked in public
for more than money
and feminist studies

She dances to understand
what a lack of love really means
for all the faces that strain to see
her lovely frame take away their money

She'll sip a Queen's elixir in New Orleans
then go to a vampire strip show in Memphis
riding heavenly lipids and a stagecoach
Lost my Baby
to a game show host
Lost my Baby
in the ecstasy of a Babylon pose

Lost my Baby
in an abstract painting
Lost my Baby
to those blue eyes of love's severity
at the lesbian committee

Lost my Baby
to a sing-a-long song
Lost my Baby
to the nation of Islam
Ah, she's walking half-naked
with her leather boots on
speaking in tongues to her Indians
dancing in a trance for hours
by the minutes
in a sentence
from a minimal mine

Lost my Baby
to a cosmic stop sign
Lost my Baby
in the innocence
of carpet burns & taking turns
playing sexy concubines

Belly Dancing

Well, the experiment failed
I've been screwing up a little bit lately
I'm running out of money
so I guess we need to talk
----hey, look here----------------------
we need to undermine the Overmind
we need to lock an egregious radio ad
in step with Deuteronomy parables
I need to exercise my active spy lifestyle
to simplify the decoder eyes
if it takes bibles & rifles & Eiffel towers
to mock the many, many menial tasks
at hand, so be it
let's get fucking busy

-but please remember I'm lazy

what's your telephone number?
and when will you be home?
preferably when time won't fold
into an clerical stopwatch
to slip into your right hip pocket
to shepherd flock it
and toss off
a Mount Zion cough
like it's rocket science
to switch composite goals
into hybrid idea clusters
when the clock is ticking

Do not waste my time.
Vaminos!

-I'm kidding, I'm joking

I saw your soul mate
selling roses by the side of the road,
he was so unhebrew
what's gotten into you?

jog, eat your vegetables
read private literature
cook eggplant lasagna
listen to ambient music
slur a sunny summer day surfboard
over verbal gurble seashells
and say it again, Sally

Sally I left my typewriter
in your blind alley
Sally I left my alley blind
in your typewriter
Sally I left my typewriter
in your alley blind
belly dancing

Sally, unless I'm in your lap,
confusing me is in your best interests

-if Engines:
there is no there there
so don't bother going there
-in the Injuns
for at least two centuries
unless the night manager lets me
blend into thin air
so I can mischievously ease
into vaguely Japanese sheriffs
daughters lover's wallets
where the honey glaze
of constant karma melts
transactions over
dead president's faces
spent on cotton candy
at a county fair
-I'd gladly raid the farm there
then there would be a there there
for me in a certain type of engine

if an Image engine
ran for power
for particular energy
purposes

I will ride the merry-go-round

(that was a billboard ad)

meanwhile, old ladies purses
are snagged by hooligans
in lieu of day jobs

I saw you hanging out
at the atom bomb factory
slobbering over antiquated
methods of thought robbery
so we must be vaguely related
stay calm but don't feel too sedated
it's not a coincidence
that psalms rhymes
with aggravated bees
that freeze willow trees
in the salty vitamin sea breeze

I'm a civil engineer of
love at first sight
victory by blind twilight
kazunteit

no days and two nights
in Atlantic city
humping a slot machine
pretending it's a time machine
belly dancing

bosses bust fat cheeks
to catch those special
bonding moments in trademarks
manufacturing a yard of aardvark cars
in shipyard arguments darting
at meme morpheme themes
haggling over Potomac learning techniques

dot, dot, so I thought, so I thought

Rapture: the president of the united states chatting
on the phone for $6 an hour to a stuttering nervous
idiot like he himself, he or me or them, that or me

-Sir, Halley's comet is coming back for customer service
and you're a worthless earthless churchless circlist
printing cursive subversive counterpoint pawns
on stock vintage stag film still frames
and passing them off as belly dancing

-wait, that's me
in fact

the facts change every time I tell the joke
I can't remember who to tell to go to hell
for kissing the Sun Nun's numb labia
uh huh, hum hum

"what am I gonna do with you, Mary Lou?"

asking for a chalice to hold change
in the dynamic of your social roles
as ass of the month calendars
and independent Gettysburg
cinema dropouts
pissing in the bucket of luck
to a rhythm schism force
of two hullabaloo quarks
wedged out of wild rice
grown from a source of love you can shove
above nudist temples you've paved
to trust the holy jabberwocky that can come
from the sticky heart of a rubber glove
in the copper penny absentia of my mind
at the center of a Britannia wishing well

waiting for a miracle to happen
I lifted a line
from a cop's cup of tea:

"If the public knew two-thirds of our officers are bunny rabbits"

talking disoriented drunks into
a mawkish legalese coma
hiding behind Tacoma
laser ray pictures
on the wall of Isis's
lexus nexus tempest

I've just recovered from a serious error
-cancel that
I'm as perfect as a calculator
naked is always accurate
I never knew I could be
so maudlin just for fun

reaching the top of a pop
god does exist
I'm so impatient
I can't sit still to resist

(you can't finish your sentences)

focus focus
relaxation
meditation
focus focus
obliterate the hopeless
focus focus
centered attention duration
patience patience

focus focus
don't talk to anyone for seven days
raise your craze
to the healthy level of (usable)
for a fixed sophist to co-mingle
with the false idols and nearly literals

-you don't really believe that shit do you?

you're not the first or last curmudgeon
in the world, go get a job
as a labor party anti-opportunist

-but I can't even tune an opportunity
I gave up all of my problems
then I pursued belly dancing

temper tantrum tantric trauma
drama dayglo dogma meter
measure teacher treasure
polo painter passion pleasure
flotsam special hassle castle
Cairo expert evening textbook
teacup lovely holiday party
Poland potluck planning syntax
falling partly cloudy clotting
body putty picture folly
belly dancing laughing
curfew camping hopping sentence
feature future higher lover lever
leader pledger hedger weather
looking better broken down
booking hello sundown sunday city
sucking sleeping sunday something
sunday sucking something slowly

suddenly something sunday special
sucking saving something sunday
loving ladder latent latter-day labor
chatter checker champion chalk talk
chutzpah chatter sunday sucking
saying something about beauty
sunday in middle earth center
satyr circle sovereign social infrastructure
inadvertently punctured with other words
that had nothing to do with the meaning
of belly dancing

-while the whole damn culture was busy
swinging around to a back ache

hacking cold cabbage in Los Angeles
has some peculiar disadvantages
over the law of averages you'd pocket
if you were only rolling along with me
to borrow some money for belly dancing

I'll imagine this 3-line newspaper ad
asking for paper tigers or plastic pogos
or manic shoeshine bags pass a tip jar
through the roof of your car
to carve a sharkskin suit
over a dark harlequin bay
in the token praise we've saved
for belly dancing

not all pretty girls plan parties in gypsy words
to take the medicine away
from your regularly scheduled program
of fudged facts & bungling acumen
about belly dancing

eternity gargles affidavits like they're cold semen
spewing Rhodes scholars into colloquial
bread basket prose collars
at steady intervals of two-past
the lovely hour of dry humping
a hungry Galapagos anecdote
about belly dancing

few words make me rattle on
about our drive-thru redemption song
as much as
(belly dancing)

bless your heart
bless your soul
I see you've found the time
to drink whiskey
a go-go
and get deified
as a pop-art mogul
snap snap snap
mister picture pose
with missus kisser
clothes la Paris so chic
so very marketable
as all the famous martyrs know
it's not what you die for
it's what style you project
when you're winning
big
when you're as far into zero
as anyone knows
as the Netherlands knows
as a weatherman knows
as a gamble goes
as far as wormholes go

you're a gold belly of Buddha
you're halfway between heaven
and a cheap deal on a motor scooter
to get you from your room in Athens
to the tombs of Attica
seen from Cessna seats in cocaine planes

(I always wanted to say that)

bad omens are filed away in a file drawer war
with 1040-EZ's, Titles, and prescription drug receipts

don't analyze parking tickets
just pay them
don't quote Socrates on a t-shirt
don't spin tin pan alley words with heavy reverb
unless you need them
(to thud with a timbre truck)

Sally
I lost my mind
in your blind alley
Sally lost her typewriter
in an alley blind
Sally I lost my blind alley
in your typewriter
Sally I lost my alley blind
in your typewriter
Sally
belly dancing
with her sainthood

Golden Pennies From Lady Luck

idea about a reduction of ideas,
ideas waning & waving out,
taking away personal belongings,
    mind erasure, rewinding
        your environment back to
           seeds,
    you've wasted too much time,
  before beginning the best day of your life
        blown in smoke rings
          to Lady Luck

before an idea about measuring
hallucinations on a typical basic
factory stock form of capturing essence
on a standardized average uniform
regular hallucination scale

flipping light switches to demonstrate
light patterns set on a switchboard,
when this room warms up god leaves,
then we can speak freely of the impending takeover,
turn on the heater, turn up the heater, hotter

please come back to see us, we love you,
give us your patently freakish impressions
of average bureaucrats crutched on old lovers
favorite bottles of denial river, mimic double agent
babble rapture scribes who practice crafts constantly
to never get it right, stealing the sight from the light,
all the right clichés, wink wink, nudge nudge,
step-by-step spontaneity, on the count of three,
one-two-three, sexercise me I am beautiful,
please pay me well, I do not work for free

I also had an idea to sell women's garments - if I were
a woman I would be an active & successful lesbian, my
art colonies would be excuses for wild Gaian orgies
with my fertile mind, what did I just say?
I would lose my mind in all that pussy
(by the way)

which may be more than an idea
about what you were thinking about
seven seconds ago
with budget codes on your lips,
gotcha.

the world boils down to psychic ad jingles,
a paper money surplus,
ideas about where to go
when you've gone flop,
when you've fucked up
in all the right places

do you expect me to buy you a drink?
an alcoholic drink?
are you waiting for a clear view & rosy skies?
more money in the bank?
I'm only listening to a drumbeat
and my specific blah blah,
I don't drink alcohol unless I'm working.

how life it is to be simple, how life it is indeed,
idea about which of these idle anxieties to demote
to a vintage retrograde, further lies lead us into early
nineteen seventy eight – an idea about yesterday,
                      thank you.

may I since I already have tomorrow?
what do I owe you?

Serrapine Jungle

Three crossed I's are all that's left
after the music died
I tried, sir, I tried
but as the electronic conscience replied:
"all guilt is manufactured,
  and that is where you're employed,
  so conjoin your fears like siamese twins"

after I'm in the holy paradigm of crisis
and the psychic effects of the 21st Century
have been identified
and I'm excited again about
my chances to win the Main course
thru a thick or thin voice
in medicines and moist
codes encoded to increase profits

-as you can imagine I'm out of money

so if you wish on a sweet chemical's name
and if your bare hands map out a frame
with a mind transformed into time
metered metaphysics is as useless
as your beaten metaphors
-unless you steal into a third element
if your vibrating pitch is elephant
whether or not this is relevant
this is beyond my control
this device has a mind of its own
so now I'm a (beaten) metaphor
so basically I'm useless

-except as a tuning fork

a day or two of serenity
in a Woman's arms charms my libido

-as you can imagine I'm out of money

Probably that old Serrapine Jungle

amazon stew brewing with plastic wrappers
and pill bottles
a silver dollar was ingested
swallowed a woodscrew
choked on formless drizzle
staring up to a pistol
muzzle-brick road whorehouse
mouthing to score Venus

Hey now, my Baby's in a commune out here, you see,
she's in one of these open country communes,
my crazy girl, she's uh, she's in one of these
garden mountains here in the country, see?

What's that formula for the drug store?
What's that formula for the drug store?

Been selling love under the uncolored neon
Glasgow Gas Glow Glass Gallery sign again?
Been selling love under the uncolored neon
Glasgow Gas Glow Glass Gallery sign again?

only a limited-edition gold christ glockenspiel
would be printed on with combat root juice deep
ingested & tingling the spine - don't pick up on Beirut
in the terminal hall posting courtroom slobber onto
coats & ties hanging in the hall

Probably that old Serrapine Jungle again

Animajade

--hello?
hey!
--yeah?
I won!
--you one?

I won a day in the sun
I knew my day would come
so I saved my soy milk bottles
for twelve years
and made mud pie crowns
out of marbled doorways
to access the pathway
to unbegun soliloquy
for my favorite stomping grounds

--is that the phrase that pays?

No, so
I poured 2000 sweatshop hours
over a two minute sound delay
and called it a day in the sun
where I was forced to stand
tied to a flagpole by my nipples
in tandem with twelve civil liberties
disappearing into none

-I was being interrogated by news parrots!

--excuse me?

I sing in a choir,
but besides the spiders
and the poltergeist snipers
I'm okay being held incommunicado
by the turnkey
like a turkey carved with avocado
play the grotto lotto is one of my many mottos

or may a mighty rains come
to the electric wheat fields
of a (guess what) stun gun
to amuse you who do
have a jokeless heart cavity
sporting orchestra boogers
on your fleece cardigan sweater
upchuck on the down stroke
versus one gracious
invitation to absolutely
quite possibly
ostensibly
soaking in vinegar
dry mouths of december

--what the fuck are you talking about?

random acts of grace are orange doorhinges
for a pair of dice hanging in paradise
not you say Hades
but to make a point
for the ladies

young lady
point to point
pant & perspire
to purify your
pair of dice

pad your heels
oh hell, here
pad your vowels

it's high time
to suffer your selves
between low shelves
silent slide shows

the porcelain lids or
the poor slim slows
I suppose

if this theatre holds
a game show persona
between the crushed velvet walls
    (and the)
grime on the grout between the tiles
arranged on the floor in the lobby
we're in trouble

earth employees drink cold coffee
like Maggie wears her
Alaskan hand-me-downs
on her other defense fence
raised on glue giddy French
raft sides to Chinese giggles
brewing in a bottom of surface tick
Asian sophistication

but I can't think clear enough
to pour your love into the kitchen sink
Babe, let me pour you a drink
let's go on to suffer
more for our do's
than our thinks

--ok...I, umm...

is another
Animajade
postcard

I'm bitter
sweet to the tongue
and I can only be left waiting
for up to two years

you start to wait now,
please keep waiting,
stop waiting,
exploit not explaining
exploring your lovers
junk drawers

sweetie I'm done
sweetie I planned
this conversation
with our tongues

sweetie meet me
at the laundry
with quarters
and dryer sheets

I'm mistaken, you dig
I made a few mistakes

--did you lose your car keys?

Dejection Specialists

….I remember you
you were my favorite
memory
you were the thought
that brought me
comfort
you had the effect
of a calming
agent
you made my mind
follow the black
thread
of plans
back home
to Afghanistan….

if a taxpayer dreams
forest in the ocean
is there a gov't to poison the world?

yes there is. people die joking about this.
just kidding, right. eh?

what you don't forget may come back to remember you
what you don't remember may come back to forget you

all rights reversed.
unauthorized copying
of this disclaimer
is strictly authorized

watch your back.
face front.

what you don't buy may come back to sell you.
of this: more later, I swear
I'm trying to mind my own damn business

if a roof falls in the ocean
is there a bureau to
keep the paperwork?

I've often wondered who's keeping track
of these important events? not me,
I'm disallowed to do such a thing

don't let facts keep you from the truth
it's always necessary to lie

….my words are not
spoken as tokens of
showbiz
or encouragement
but of
condescending
bitter rancor
and personal digs
at your character
  -thematic
   thuggery
just kidding
about something
copyright 1986
dejection specialists….

Noetry Extempore

poetry is no
no poetry
poetry is famous
for poetry no

poetry extempore
is what you might expect
poetry no to be

poetry shouters
no poetry

poetry soul
wrong poetry
martyr chopped
liver river water

poetry holy
poetry no no

poetry bath
no poetry

poetry institution
pretty shit body
no poetry no poetry

poetry rush
no poetry

poetry corporation
poetry no
poetry cock spooky
this is poetry

no poetry not poetry
pottery

poetry alias
no poetry

poetry intoxication
poetry no

poetry magic seizure
a mind cough
poetry not

poetry gestation
not poetry

poetry map
poetry no

poetry god federal
italicized moans
no poetry

poetry ruins
poetry no
poetry jigsaw
not poetry

poetry symbol example
people numbers sun
no poetry
poetry image

no poetry
poetry package
poetry clot

poetry knot
poetry bottle engine
shot cannot is
poetry kraut

poetry sexual
no poetry
poetry shovel
no poetry no
poetry the green
promise eater
not poetry

poetry auger
no poetry
poetry expression
not poetry
poetry catastrophe
quixotic mucous membrane
poetry yes

bootleg poetry
is the only poetry

elegance
is an over rated word
anyway you slur it

-please disregard all these things

*Poetry in pursuit
of that cheap
catch-all phrase*

Tiny Futures (atomic center)

No

    (bad Lord jokes
        at a posh
          Dutch emporium)

The Princess herself is sitting up
on the top shelf of liquor bottles,
let's approach her like a news reporter
would reach into a folder-

dear inner feminine self:
I have no qualms about breaching you
on any subjects you wish to discuss
and I will always blow private kisses to you
-I'm hip
-and I am a very passionate man, yes

so lets get down to brass tacks
and how much do you want for a bottle
of your flowing love?

I need some yin to balance my yang

I will always be aware of you, me
my drifting continent within
and by extension
I drag me
to a state of simple

-*help!*

no none of these
no nothing
no empty
no no
mojo syntax mirror
know no
know empty
know nothing
know none of these

if you walk from fingertip
to big toe
you go
from irrelevance
to obscurity
in one fell swoop
of ghost written
business cards
yard arms
and tax write-offs

young and fleshy calculators
cow cow powers

Jung beautiful lung
spring water drum
twenty racket noise
twenty floors
below us
make sense
and make a damn fine
throbbing meat puppet
drift into cosmic slop space
to play for maiden's milk

-to take a little bit of the dream away for one's self

-just a little bit of peace for yourself

take a little bit of your own hyperlexia
to get you through
drive-thru liquor store
clerk interviews

take a little bit of bitterness
to get you through 12
dead-end jobs in one tax season

whoa, dude
that's more than enough
rhyme timing
to get your mouth engine
apologizing
for all that philosophizing
you been applying
to sports drinks
with advanced carbohydrates

dear atomic centre core:
on the bible code do you swear
that you hear coordinated musical scales
played in opposition to compositions
that are designed to flesh out
entropy holes in new world myths?

and is Shelly really picking
up seashells by the seashore
or is T.S. Eliot just a rogue meteorite
striking the earth just right
for grocery stores
to stay open 24 hrs a night?

is it ok to capitalize on the things you like?

(or) am I just jewing the facts
apart in art for the sake of sacrificing
my part in the play of life as a cardinal sin
that stops and starts and begins again
and ties together any other loose ends
that fit in one way or another?

Miss Mary wanna come
away with me to paradise
we'll make the world obey a come
by our own frantic schedules
-We'll be deportees

-but really I've become
a damn drag to hang out with
it's like I've gone native
with the Mossomog nation

-I work with the world
over a truckload
of salt & snow
and thrift store fools gold

 -when I wuz just a baby-child
I sang along with communist party
phrases and felt simply amazing

-and as my salad days increased by threes,
greased lightning laid flat
every forest in the trees

-vanity psychedelia leanings paid for themselves
by symbolizing my internal struggles with creative
campaigns against the processed suggestions
of modern life

I'm feeling like an end-times atavistic farmer
not yet farming his own future
but soon the future will be over

oh you,
you act like the fate of the world
rests on whether people combine
their talents with a sensical spirit of mind
that tries to bind together our scattered tribes
before swallowing thumbtacks in public
becomes a full-blown social movement

oh you,
raising many weird questions in west Texas
to men whose job it is to keep the quota sheep
spending marked money only in particular pastures

oh you,
you stand outside the doors of holy public places
and make comical faces with shifting eyebrows
to arouse your own soul to walk down the red carpet
to the base of an emotional monument
for believing in your own idiosyncrasies

and for a minute and a half you happily cried
for all the right reasons, and you stirred the wind
of the seasons you walk in
out of the soles of your feet
then you said in ancient Greek:
"now beliefs may go to sleep"

and I said "go mad again, like beef,
beat the emcee's ignorance blisters
with buttered tofu"

and then you said "there you go again, going"

and I really felt like playing arpeggio clusters
on my Hondo - but my guitar only has 2 strings
and I never learned to play an instrument that didn't
insist on playing me first

I am an errand boy of the partial semi-thought
I have no philosophically fixed positions, except that
I won't budge from my position of no philosophically
fixed positions - I use words from the pawn shop of the
soul, organized under a ghetto rainbow

so what to do?
you never seem to be comfortable
unless old habits are breaking or you're
pasting a compulsion in a pyrex petri dish
growing a walk-talk biosphere
in a brick oven solarium

you verbally mock a padlock
binding a set of closed circles
locking you in with habeas corpus plates
holding a memorial service inside a breadbasket
full of wine and subliminal advertisements based on
blocking concentric circles only on the outside of
squares to continue spinning cautious halos
inside the mighty nowhere

for all this means is to rephrase a question
I guess I'm better at attacking arguments
than I am at raiding memory banks to
question my five point system
of finally almost finishing

-something

and when I finally ask you what any of this means
(detangling a pocketful of popes & kings & queens)
you look at me like I've gone loopy crazy on themes
like I'm wired and you're cool, calm & collected
just as you announce the poem has performed
just as you'd expected
and now I see you're waiting for me
to be my own version of you
who can be whomever they are to be you
and I say that's what it means for you
to see me be me

(I just caught myself catch myself talking to myself)

hey hey, my my
your mind is fried
on ghost stories blowing
like gale-force winds
about love's eternal
patent pending alarm clock
seen as a pair of nature-loving
Prussian-born ambient god minds
wishing you well
by sending your ass to jail
for hatching plots
against progress
by sworn testimonies
and perjuries to the Fuzz
and an almost
deliberate probably
way of setting your life up
for a philosophy of all that ever was

just imagine yourself
picking up trash after yourself
36 hrs a day

how do you change a formula
that has been used for two weeks
as a reference guide for biting tongues
with obsessive /compulsive endings
that never quite end due to syntax
magic that attaches words to every
blank space you will ever see?

never ever sever the better weather lever
that links customs to suicide
you might fall up to heaven
with heavy baggage
and god will kick your sorry ass out

"...damn, I never expected that..."

do you see showers flowers
towers powers stars cars
jars guitars attics manics
panic lingo
balloons in your stomach
marble teeth
billions of little supers?
Tiny futures?

Not Me.

II / Serve The Creative Impulse, Idiots

Volunteer to mentor peat moss.

I'm Like, So Full of Shiite

young people
can't imagine
the physical
f   o   r   m
of the definitive
sheepherder
until he closes the gate
on his flock
and locks the door
behind him

oh, now you're locked in
oh, now your imagination springs into action

fifty-seven million americans
living twenty-seven seconds too late

eighty-billion americans
can't be wrong about beer & huge tits
but can they be
excused from
sunday services?

god never serves food
on good dinnerware
when we're at the table

when I asked god why,
god referred me to another ego fable
about privileged minds shading over Indian id
with the ugly karmic morass of the white man's
casual day leisure suit

-nice shoes

Serve the Creative Impulse, Idiots

Once, or twice maybe, I was a superhero detective named Jeffery in an unpublished novella I wrote while living in a one bedroom cottage on a small Greek island. No, actually I didn't write anything when I stayed there. I've never been to Greece. I was thinking about super-collider flyers that pass you on the highway to Dallas only, not nostalgia. I might agree with some of that. But I don't have to read modern philosophy or study Egyptian hierarchies to know that.

See, I'm already employed to the void.

Please tell me what your question was. Am I the reason young girls break out of their rooms at night to attend community college? I doubt it, but my analyst tells me I have no effect on strangers. My peace cube hubris is still strong, strung together with juxtaposition glue of a fixed-star position that sells sensitive newspapers to us to read and we enjoy them. It's very nice. Polar hands in my pockets, jingling change. Opening and closing a pocketknife, but not in a Christopher Walken walking away kind of way.

Art, apart from distracting us from real life, also helps to enhance our real life failures. This is my favorite part of the leisurely stroll past a shelf of books. I feel that empty miserly grumble of creative hunger in my smug, blue collar, working american life. So it's nice to sing loudly when I don't have any disposable income to shoot fun from. Only pendulums whisper like parrots to a stack of scratched records. Remember that.

Stop, begin with a pause and continue sporadically. Finish your spiel with victorious grunting and orgasmic facial expressions. Afterwards, claim to be genuinely articulate on the subject of "gorge chortles." Then have a hidden track in your writing for after the applause dies down. Oh, and be prepared for a real drag on your drone scrotum: at least you know that was funny.

Run-off grooves never lie. Grace under a restraining order, you are a child of the new kingdom and I may never be so beautiful again. A fused corroborating memory booth with six arresting officers and audiotape. Two more bridges burned across the river Kwai detox clinic. Hotbox tourniquets, terror & fear as you sign your name to a gov't petition for public lecture space. You just might get the podium.

Lime is a priceless flavor agent, a double-agent in time not to be trusted in a crisis. Limerick, dome fodder, ah, now we're getting somewhere. Truant brew hydra tea, sorry about the petty pussyfooting. Oh this beverage tastes marvelous. Golf huge in deluxe bastions of sewage. Draw a staggering post-pills pope. Yes, yes the preambling leads to a slap on the face. Kiss me. Give me a report on the motives of neanderthal juries in cases of hipster sophistication.

I want to be sold as a stand-in for avant-garde ripoff exploitation. I drive a mazda truck. Pull me into any areas graying into that publicity machine. Zone off unfactual misnomers. And I want to be regarded as an Elvis Presley look-alike. On the double. This will add more flavor to my later memoirs, no matter what I lie about.

I like severe weather. It really brings folks together, and people work well together when they have to. Fear and a tight focus is all it takes to keep the bad johnson's from noticing me. I never get pegged as a deliberate purveyor of vanity psychedelia manifestations when coastlines are being wiped out by a hurricane. I also appreciate the smell of a city after heavy rain, reminds me of why I pay taxes.

I saw a cheesy slogan written in my captain's logbook. I won't repeat it here. Actually I will, if you read that sentence backward. I guess it depends on what kind of employment mood you wear. I will not copy job codes in Arabic fractal bones, sir, until my lawyers commit their signatures to my release papers.

I'll give you a minute to condense many words into a math quiz: tongues of fish, a pool of genes mixing DNA strands and strains of sand in a classical string concerto, emphasizing small village publications.

Street maxims vibrate between your tonsils. She had her tonsils removed. She's my favorite author of a lost cause, lost because I've misplaced her xeroxed soul exchange. I'm noticing patterns again. Revolution, yawn, fight tyrannical state power, hit the snooze button, sleep nine more minutes. Relax. Do you accept Jeesus Chrysler as your personal savior, with a low 9.8% APR? If the deal includes a free ticket to heaven, with a three day stay – all meals paid, I'll join the herd.

Bird, Bird, have you heard the word?
I heard that LIVE on the Asperger Syndrome show.
My spiritual declaration will be followed by a
smorgasbord of meaty gut pulp sautéed
with shiitake mushrooms, meade and street wheat.

Wow - baby armageddon, psychic insurance provisions,
legal fuck clause, key chapters printed in invisible ink.

I've said this before and I will say it again: Surprise,
revolution, yawn, fight tyrannical state power,
hit the snooze button, sleep another nine minutes.
How may I help you? Good morning! Looking Good!
Have A Good Weekend! Icon! Grooving youth image!
Style! Style! Slang particulars! Drug syndicate child!

Fruity color additives enrich salt crystal money.
-that's a story I would read part of, if I had to.

If I am allowed to have 34 sanctions against this nation,
I will first say this: Individual over the nation,
remember that. Do yourself a reminder, if you would
have to. Don't remember yourself, remember my
country 'tis of thee. Remember mixed messages.
Remember how long to boil your tea.

Serve the creative impulse, Idiots. Volunteer to mentor
limestone principle seekers. Get actively involved with
peat moss. Why must you always insult me with scams
that can't catch me? I breathe on a pun barrel and never
say the same thing once.

Twice you have lied to your Superiors with the intent of
a secret C---- tryst. You have a black mark beside your
name. I'll remember you for Garden of Eden real estate
escrow. I'll see that you make good on your promises to
pay me money. You can send your first check to me
c/o *Handshakes & Daggers Inc*. I didn't need that extra
rib anyway. It made me cough like a hung jury. I'm glad
you're here, Sweetie. I'll make a few calls, see what I
can't do.

Boom Boom. Ground bass above the tree line. A tiny future window pane on a 12th floor apartment building has a daily viewing of *"How glass breaks,"* an educational film produced in the early 70's. It is projected from the window in the afternoon when there is a rope swing to automatic god access, 15 cents a minute.

But I'll save you some time-
Lick the roof of your mouth,
you're an automatic mystic

Back to Abacus

back to back track lagging shack hack
sack to back facts runs laps shaps dags
rock hot jaw the law sack back to back
to back rack haggle lag holy spazz fat lat
to sat lat lat lat lat to back hats bind hall
news jall climb blind on one side
fine lines enthrall call enough
to euphoria back to back
to back ball tall dig hig to wig shig explain
sig fig to rig jets lets bets to wood
iron nest sets hets libby shun shine thin
gin to redemption hallow Sally
Salt Lake City jolly old bat
back to back to back folly dome pall
call linked loddy shod shine shin
shake shark shifty shake to find liberty
liaisons linked to luggage gods
shameless jells bells blem blithe
time on time on time synchronized
show up shaw shall back remain
bald back to back to back
arm in hand hammer jams javes
drinking cold water grows galls
syllable sawn sall sang some songs
saw the same sold son of something
something something please
sun deliver us clean clear
back to back to back identification
with antimatter position molecule
divide in rug bender pline pine
math methodist magazine drifter
back to back to back alley
watch water blem vide shaggy
done decadence back to back to back

Go Spies Go!

mushroom eyes
bugged-out in bed

custom-painted
flat tire pliers

Chicago theatres
and project cricket
plastics

act detached
about our sour
wasted world
and smile

oh the guilt
is just horrendous

yankee acres
demo tapes
taxi lanterns

acrobatic oak ashtrays

gaudy macho root pocket women
loving subtly dead men
who slap on slim
pinstripe suits
with jungle juice scented
misogyny perfumes
to go get loose
at used car salesman bars

-a blow-out sale of repossessed issues with faulty fuses

Or the madman adman says:
Tonight, news at 11:00 PM:
　　Simulated Immaculate Conception
　　viewing booths
　　rented by credit card

don't feel shame
over your favorite
folk shack jamboree
protest poem

just read it to me
I won't laugh
I will only -

-dig that plumbing!

oh, the guilt
is wrapped up tightly

black black airs
voting paltry
peasant agendas
back to abacus
digits on your
Rockefeller
ring finger

(you'd)

bloody better be there
better be waiting
with napkins
and a spooner
junket pumpkin
lilac bag of fuck you

I have a permit
to solicit
raw ideas
from the diplomat
of the laundromat

pastrami sandwich
statesman fines
are paid in double time
triple tickets
for washing nature
in a construction
zone

if you think we live
in troubled times
you haven't
prayed
for immigration cards
to Poncho Villa
or Liberty Allah Jolly Roger
without funneling cash into
dot dot dot
ad campaign
torpedoes

you paid for free time in Arizona
and got bit by the Santa Anna clause
of Corona Extra

tasty tax
pasted packs
of marlboro
cigarettes
cough cough
sucker sucker

organize noise
into a central
voice of no
choice no
voice no
noise no
central no
noise plan

the statistical man
image controller
stuck in staccato
algorithms
of equal or lesser value
to the local lord
pouring surveillance
thru his window

-read the cue card, dipshit

heeeeeere's Johnny Mofo:

once a beacon of sexy youth culture
now serving 15 years in a California prison
for misquoting a SWAT team commander's
come-on lines while agents were burning scrambled
eggs and messages in his small kitchenette:

> *"do you know how many cops it takes*
> *to shove a man*
> *down a flight of stairs?*
> *none.*
> *the man fell.*
> *now, be patriotic & pass the maple syrup"*

ah, remember the days
gee whiz miss america
I sure miss my artistic licenses

soda pop teen dream dime shops
top my list of hot stop
places to pause for a few paces
and castigate a greasy carpenter
about his jury duty record
or his allegiance to the flag

time to mention guilt
again

now I hear your thoughts
with both eyes

oh, the guilt is singing
amazing
grace

and yes it does pay to advertise
to common ties that bind

> *"...I made $33,000 in two days by catering*
> *food to the film set of a popular TV show!*
> *Who knew thinly-sliced meats & imported cheeses*
> *with crackers & pimento would pay me more*
> *money in 2 days than my old state job would pay*
> *for a whole year! This is the American dream!"*

I know where I get *my* information these days
(from a *286G-Vortex 9th Sense Cognition Reader*)

(go spies go!)

Transcription of the August Step Dehydrate Tape

1.
[first sound you hear is a tape recorder clicking on. then a frothy rumble that cuts to machinery noise and a nearby stranger asking an imperfect joke or two]

   -click-

hey! I'm looking
   for the guy who shot my paw

do you know what an elephant uses for a
tampon?
               a lamb

[sound of air being sucked like money. a microphone rubs against a phone call. I encounter a rip-off artist]

   good morning sunshine
   early in fervor
   I ask a favor
   I hope you can deliver

ha, choose yes.
it's a virus, maybe some kind of illness.
a rope of whisper between seedy and that bowl.
continually still.
mister foster, lobster.
sixteen bridesmaids in the closet.
sixteen modes of mars august step dehydrate.
nerves spin art.

forming a grand jury when town locals bib kabob.
are you sure? cause it.
august step noise legures.
sixteen awnings forming a grand jury. just to be sure.
hare krishna conceived that little voice.
what the hell is that? you know.

[coughing]

hey!
who ever gave you permission to laugh?

*[whirring - seven bubble percentages
spliced to plant face]*

*...no, that would survive if you lose them right in the head.
very few people fuckin live to see...*

metaphysics for sale! for sale! orgasm donor, owner!
held in high regard it's not hard to fly without wings!
but it's cartoons to skip Egypt babe!

2.
> [*lost wallet - $56, andromeda bubble*
> *percentages, my first chaotic ballet*]

do you promise?
do I promise?
yeah.
well what do you think?
you hope I play this?
adam? adam?
does that sound familiar?
adam? adam?
does that sound familiar?

did you call me a fungi?
yes, you're a funny guy.
you're too kind to me

adam you got your protest last time adam
adam you got your protest last time adam
iguana week adam
iguana week adam
huh?
you know the rules adam
iguana week
twisting an adam
twisting an adam
adam clip kiss

you won, adam
oh thank you
I love you
I love you too
bye
bye

3.
> *[world harp harp harp, a world away*
> *for less than minimum wage]*

of course you start to mouth...
of course you start to mouth...
quick quiz:
don't be a square, hang a louie?
did anyone ever tell you you're useless?
when was the last time you were
knocked unconscious?
within a basic red square?
rain kept running out?

from yo-yo mops to telephone tops

> *good morning sunshine*
> *early in fervor*
> *I ask a favor*
> *I hope you can deliver*

yeah!
panels, no. whoa. D chord.
funnel drums to third intro.
I like the way the tape plays
before it records.

> *[clearing of the throat]*
> *[the throat is clear]*

> *perfectly natural*
> *breaking my fever*
> *play a little sadness*
> *over our faces*
> *to hush our favorite rites of passage*

4-a.
> *[static laughs: competing for an open-palm Frampton radio rhythm on the hood of a '78 monte carlo]*

suicide is not funny. suicide is not funny.
suicide is not something to joke about.
you should not joke about suicide.
suicide is not funny.
of all the things that make me laugh,
suicide is not one of them.
if you hear a funny joke, chances are
it's not about suicide.
you could kill yourself quite easily
with a small handgun.
   (oh won't you show me the way)
if you committed suicide it would not be funny.
   (I want you to show me the way)
suicide is for weak minded.
one thing that is not funny is suicide.
you are pathetic. weak minded.
you are weak minded & suicidal.
   (oh won't you show me the way)
suicide is for the weak minded.
   (I want you day after day)
no, you're not just paranoid
or imaging things.
people really are watching you
and mocking you
and making fun of you.
weak minded. you want
to smile, don't you?
after all, it's all laws or swimsuits.
   (I want you day after day)

        [cue belly laughter]

okay, I'll get serious now.
sacrifice. a bright sunny day.
sacrifice. iced tea. get a good job.
in lieu of four words. I can help you.
identify. sacrifice. kill. yourself.
not killing just anyone. you.
kill, yourself. stop drinking
my water. die. go away.

good morning sunshine
early in fervor
I ask a favor
I hope you can deliver

how do you know that you
are you?
how could you possibly know
that you know?
you can be instantly dead.
a life strategy for sale by owner.
top hat, cabbage hands.
you don't exist.
suicide is not funny.
suicide is not something you
should joke about,
unless you're serious.
suicide wouldn't be funny, per se.
Cadillac's are funny though.
just plain old Cadillac's.
no goddamn Cadillac modifiers.

4-b.
> *[I also remember recording*
> *cellophane firecrackers*
> *on my handheld womb,*
> *but it wasn't really all that much fun]*

you are very easily influenced by new jersey.
that little voice telling you. love yourself.
love yourself.
   (belch)
kill yourself.
you're your own enemy.
love your enemy.
kill yourself.
most people hate you,
god especially.

keep your chin up, idiot.

> *[this was a public service announcement]*

5.
> *[this is the part of the tape scheduled*
> *to not have a later bracketed intro]*

are you thirsty?
got any to roll?

I know what you can roll - your window up!

just cruise cuz I gotta roll this up
then we gotta sm-m-m-moke it

> *[suggestions duly noted]*

Greek sandwich, in parenthesis.
heroin, in parenthesis.
torn jeans, in parenthesis.
a job interview, in parenthesis.
parenthesis J., in parenthesis.
it's fun and just right for you.
you're special. overdose.
needles. veins. overdose.
those aren't my pants.

now what, misanthrope?
I'll tell you won't dig from a coma.

6.
> *[played to the tune of an economy wig]*

a working economy is a sure wig to field in newspeak, vis-à-vis dome karma I told you about yesterday. the price of a mud tunnel student's non-profit elbow of america is rising. I stand beside you and congratulate you to attract a strong labor market. it is in my spine to support an entire generation of political activists toward a meteor shower. so as I pass this note hand to hand, please remember how I am. and the next time you see a scientist in a police uniform issue a ticket gratis, weep. how many layers of private jokes can I leave out? as it will always be safe to produce a terminology of many careers. believe in what you feel is underlying your bare feet. walk into a big gimmick of wars and napalm bombs, centuries, history. hair bibles split, I'm tired. isn't it a fitting tribute to the work busting backs of men and women and children? I enlighten myself to what you are, and I may never find my hand again.

hey fuck you
how's your highball?
nice to see you.
yeah. have a day.
alright, cute frisbee
let's talk by the train platform, under my underwear.
did you know my name is a populist popsicle?

oonisms. isms. croak. keys. isms.
ah, grease generator.

7.
> *[the only commercial, apparently I opened a can of funny]*

you've been acting kind of weird.
do you have feelings of guilt?
isolation? hopelessness?
have you been hearing voices?
of course not.
been hearing voices?
of course not.
been hearing these voices.
no, of course not.
you're crazy.
but are you?
a gimmick?
been hearing these voices.
you're not the real you.
been telling you to.
what you may believe to be you.
what you think. whispering.
of course, it's your imagination.
this is only part one. rejoice.
you're confused.
I recall this was a bit of a rush.
it totally occurred to me, apparently still.
just a corner few left.

....yeah, on thermal drive. about 60 hours a week.

a glow you fuse your eye, catch.
I can't bitter spill, so.
see ya later 1996.
I've been coughing up blood.
where've ya been?
coughing up blood.
quaff these blood stains.

handsome idle idol.
moat flares.
these blood.
does been hiding.
dust bin. blood.
teach king cater.
wine kings. blood.
I've been coughing up blood.
where but?
coughing up blood.

[ill-sounding coughs added for effect]

that was my integrity on the floor.
you already walked over it.
no, just forget it.
it's too late for me to plan
on entertaining you
the "right" way
constantly.
deep pockets for my
secret warehouse keys.
jingling.

8.
> *[a snap of one-way conversation from a news media office intern, issued as a misnomer]*

no, I'm just gonna toss this tape into a box full of older tapes when I'm done, and quickly get rid of the box, probably to goodwill or salvation army.

you won't tell the girls I was joking about coughing up blood & suicide skits will you? cuz they don't find that stuff very attractive and neither do I, see. hey I'm bored, let's go driving around with balloons & aqua tanks. I'm too tired for regular sitting around I'm uncomfortable.

9.
> *[tape ends, sounds much like a tape ending]*

-click-

Egyptian Reverb

I flunked out of a creative writing knitting club
just because I disappear in my own pictures
and I can't be trusted with paradigm shifts
because I can't resist going gaga

saved my subtle changes in an old briefcase
lost my luck in my luggage
in two thousand miles of rainy castle maps

crooks stumbling in doorjambs
broadcast over pirate radio
still going strong after all these years

and I'm still naked as a
jack-of-spades with the queen
of hearts

arrested in paradise
sentenced to 12 weeks
of reading Tom Clancy
for harboring an idea about
13 visual superstitions
in Philadelphia
against the advice of
a nurse who looks
at me calmly as she
dispenses my pain medications to me
-my pain medications back to me
-for a moment the nurse looks
like a girlfriend from interior Mexico
the woman who taught me how to cook
a mean tortilla soup
who showed me how to sew buttons
back onto my shirts

-I remember how she never wanted
to sit with me and sing Hanukah jingles
or taste Norwegian lingual soap
cranked from a gramophone phonograph
that I saw in a photograph

-in another dream
we order dark suede jackets
from a swank London catalogue
we were talking in widgets
walking in extended circular paths
around the village baths that cleanse
old soul Indians of European descent
-did I say that?
-that I get passed to them in conversations
intercepted by the lord of gargoyle integers
and self-righteous taxpayers of the first world
bankers contract?

-spiritually binding?

but in the first place
we have her beautiful face
asking me
for a cup of tea
and a James Joyce
junk pile of cheese

and all I have is erstwhile
interests and boredom
- enthusiasm!

she sucker punches me in my sleep
and I dream about the living chamber
in my pyramid filling with dirty water
-I'm alive!

A Peruvian Love Song

ain't nuthin but a rainy haze
a dry tick-tock upon an oily freeway
this highway ain't nuthin but a dirty
den of thieves
and a business man grins & says

"check please"

a pocket *I Ching*
ain't nuthin but a series
of 64's & 6 three's
a blue blurry-eyed cross
between a hotspot on the earth
and a universal first time for everything

a beating of blinds
burns my eyes
and signals a council to begin
a dark star chart that guides
mankind's why's & when's
and wince if you will
but hey! it's as simple as that
to clap - it's flat & it's hat
and it's green & it's grove
and it's great & it's grat
and that vaudevillian fact
comes up the jersey turnpike
and turns left into your childhood
and from that flows a path
of woes & throes to bat
out to third base
as gemini clouds congregate
and play the wine cellar clear
from Canada….

....to a great wide sky in the plywood
and a marble floor
a knock-knock-knock upon the door
and a friendly wave goodbye

goodbye

oh, it's all over now baby blue
she's leaving tomorrow
on a train from Boston
to Ecuador & Peru

and you?
ah, you're always hanging around
cleaning off these goddamn tables

are you able to entertain us
in any other way than these
endless fables?

can you cast your shadow over the moon
and reuse that effect
to gauge & direct
any city you choose into no poet's dirty little hands?

must strangers be the finest examples on drafting tables
of mad castle candle park satellites?

(so)

whatever seems right seems alright with me
ain't nuthin but free & free is free
ain't nuthin but a few minutes of your time
ain't nuthin but free & free is free is alright

Protecting Intellectual Property by Giving It Away Free

100 ideas appeared out of nowhere

1 Errant bombs, woops, dropped on peasant villages
2 Automatic Jesus visages
3 The only noteworthy pratfall to fall back up your Aristocratic nose
4 Misfiled with Consater
5 Don't feel comfortable
6 If paperwork falls on a forest in a roof is there a bureau to keep the ocean?
7 The Move Big Arson Caper
8 No business like shoe business
9 Disc Jockey debauchery
10 Yes, but the eggs crack every time I tell the yolk
11 Money Beats Soul
12 Sterling digits mock modal models of time symbols
13 Go on calmly
14 Japanese Mexican Germans
15 No more cosmic jive, shut up
16 Niccr
17 Facts will fall apart for good entertainment
18 Work Morning Night Foundation
19 Loper proper
20 Don't let facts keep you from the truth
21 Will Loudcloud dust my gloves?
22 With kind permission, I may never find what I'm looking for
23 Disco Quaker Acres
24 Isn't it an obvious boogie?
25 I'm dropping my harpoon
26 Bitter End lingo
27 A tiny Yucatani argument

28 The crew from Leicester confer,
   the tennis racket mesh atrophied
29 Psychic health jokes
30 Cop pockets
31 Tomato cage pages
32 I'm falling in love with stop signs
33 The Funk conspiracy
34 Darwin said something about survival
35 Surprise: your gov't hates you
36 Cement symptoms
37 A thousand miles of melody
38 If a taxpayer dreams forest in the ocean is there a gov't to poison the world?
39 Extracted grooves from the antebellum
40 Rotary modules govern intake compression
41 What you don't buy may come back to sell you
42 It's raining everywhere but here, and I'm fine miserable on old patio furniture
43 Mannered tasks
44 Important global character assassination
45 What you don't know may come back to know you better
46 This is neither complete or edited (nor edited?)
47 Miniature golf in the valley of broken language
48 Reprint of anonymous text written on sex advert left at an apolitical demonstration
49 Exploring interruptions
50 Unlimited Froth goes commercial
51 Being verbally abused by a foreign tongue
52 Bubblegum of doom
53 If a cellphone rings in the forest is there a consumer to say hello?
54 This message explodes
55 Plotted glaciers
56 Endless grief the color of love

57 Across leather seats
58 Manifest Destiny Festivities
59 Numb aplomb: a plumber & a nun
60 What you don't quit may come back to start you
61 Colloquial minimalism
62 Nutritional press conference
63 You weird fuckers
64 Pimping my karma
65 Price fix? what's the special occasion?
66 Marmalade interludes with Andy Spam
67 You are not welcome here
68 The most dangerous joke
69 Freedom Except
70 The key to success
71 Insurance disputes & pipe bombs
72 This hour hurts better
73 If a roof falls in the ocean is there a bureau to keep the paperwork?
74 Robe fish, rope dish, rogue wish
75 None bottoms up spill a glass of zeal/French petticoat revue
76 Nuclear banjo
77 Unraveling the American yarn
78 Miniature Revolution in the Suburbs
79 Another red film
80 In sync to an ice rink, a frozen yell sunk in
81 Happy tourniquets right here look!
82 Oceans of Wurlitzer skronk
83 Gene's blue random jam
84 Unlimited Froth Appreciation Society
85 Transcription of organ donor music
86 No use owl-my proxy apology season format takes a turn for the better

87 A thousand deaths in the lions mouth and one phoenix rising to appeal to bibliophiles
88 Rattle of Amish ice-cream
89 A day of conferences and podium backwash makes wick eyes veterans of crunches
90 Rainy day eye movements for groove soldiers, baby
91 Unnaturally happy
92 Austin is not a proper way to describe a stomach ache, but to drink air is not it either
93 Waking up from a yen sleep to a flak jacket is too much & calls for radio silence
94 Planets of Bags
95 Never again will there be a media extravaganza
96 Arching midwives
97 America is Over, Operators are standing by
98 Unbegun
99 Hi, I'm literally a Sofa
100 Just like a kitchen sink, an Idea doubles in size and rejects its own meaning

Imitation of a Newspaper Column

I found your loaded signature in yesterdays newspaper
and I reprinted it on 26 flash cards
to constantly refresh my memory index
and now I feel sick

and perhaps I should apologize to you in person
but I don't know where I am
so I'll send you a message of cracks and crumbs
and cabbage from the folds of my sticky psyche

you'll hear a devout blast of choral trumpets
blowing my last call for air in a time seizure window

fragmented melodies play back together
much easier from a comfortable chair

-so relax

welcome to a concert program of repeated
musical burps, listen or leave, or be gone

or believe this is my first impression
of myself after seeing myself
at the end of a pointed finger

as if I must explain
my Jewish breath complex
related to 1930's newsreels
& clusterfucked ideals
(I watched Woody Allen movies as a kid)

oh, my burn-out fears
I still make wishes inside
vaginal theatres

moans of indulgence
blowing smoke
behind two-way Kozik mirrors
-I am speaking of an emotion
that only approaches love
but never bothers love

I'm serious, frequently
I'm waaaay too loose
I'm a luddite progressive
oh, I'm so self-induced

I drank too much swampland
I talked language down to number 1
I'm not afraid to say any
combination of words
I'm only afraid of my need
to say those words in court

but isn't that because god
makes philosophy fall short
of the working man's dirty shirt?

OUCH we say and close that book properly
a symphony of love for propaganda's daughter
she is married to a helicopter company
suddenly sunshine is dripping
from my moribund cacophony

I lied to myself, I lied on camera
I lied to my blank canvas
I had lunch with a rote anecdote
I moved like on automatic
I'm archived with creosote
and a gallon of dry fission paste,
so sue me

imitate a liberal base of fanatics
press the hunger button in your mouth
to cut down the rain forests in the clouds

watch a clock go bicycle
inside a pterodactyl

even a broken clock is right
twice a day
ding dong

and then I realize today is friday
and I am wrong about everything
I know

How could I make these things up?

Pellagra, for example
is a disease caused by
a niacin deficiency in the diet
characterized by skin changes
nerve dysfunction
and mental symptoms

-mental symptoms
like what?

well, the higher authorities did not specify
so I remain vague

-should I get a crude booster shot?

no, but we should all read the newspaper together

I'm Dropping My Balloon

I'm dropping my balloon
    and I refuse to pick it back up.
I'm protesting the picking-up of dropped balloons.
    Well, I'm protesting the picking-up
of a dropped balloon
    by the person who dropped it.
A dropped balloon is for a person unrelated
    to the balloon-dropper to pick up.

Loose balloons being picked-up in public places
by artistically unmotivated people
works to incite a ritualistic
reawakening of our inner longing
to engage in sustained acts of novelty.

Today balloons, tomorrow inquisitive mind bombs.

Dropping balloons & the chain of events that follow
allow me to have my pie and eat my cake too, which
is a good reason to have a balloon mitzvah that misses
the yes-men and impresses the Ladies.

I am also very interested in water balloons
    for obvious reasons.
Although, even water balloons include a few
    spoonfulls of feathery interruptions
        (feeble clarity)
So anyway, getting back to balloons
    and the balloon entelechy…
        …balloons boom spirit
            back to basics.*

*a last-minute chance to voluntarily pick-up a balloon.

Zapruder Clap Track

life's occult! life's occult!
a Cambrian cult rhythm
cult encoded, cult encrypted
cultured cheese culture cults
private cultures
hiding in private
vulture cults

cult dreams of cult seeding
digging a cult beating
cleaning cult acrylic floors
peeling thru a cult ceiling

a whiplash flash holds your tongue
to take a throat culture
you say the words of cult edifice
said for the sake of a greater cult science
in pursuit of lofty cult creamings

cults come! cults go!
cults come! cults go!
cultured cheese culture cults
quick cult vicious
sneeze! cough!
caught in a cult office
screening cult xerox

cutthroat cults crept into bed
with cult diamond eyes
cut cult climates of wealth
cult wealth cut well with sirens
cult sirens chide us all
into cult-minded & cult-sided flaws

I'm occult! I'm occult!
of cold candy cast through
cold cult Kennedy candy
cults flats!

You're occult! You're occult!
of cold candy cast past
cold cult Kennedy candy
cults flats!

That's occult! That's occult!
of cold candy cast into
cold cult Kennedy candy
cults flats!

Life's occult! Life's occult!
of a cult image cut flat

III / Dig Big Baggy Grotto Mob Mottos

No More Miracles (Miracles No Mas).

For Good Golly Miss Molly's
Late Night Poetry Class

A perennial tune in the tome of her dreams
is the smell of the tomb of Tutankhamen

Sure, I like brunettes and redheads and blondes.
Hair dyed in unnatural colors can be sexy too.
Blue doesn't scare me. English teachers arouse me.
But mostly I just like a woman's style

good golly Miss Molly, you're blooming now

what's a palm tree without a spare key?
what's a golf club without an overdub?
what's a teen sensation without adult fornication?
what's a full time job without early morning fog?
what's a fork in the road without a spoon for code?
what's a liquid diet without an ounce of crazy glue?

I have every reason to jump off the 12th St bridge
I have every reason to cringe when I pay my phone bill

leaves of satin, milk of peace
I still have 50,000 missing pieces

you can say that you are careful
but that doesn't make you special
in the city limits
props
in the little city
frogs
in Chinatown
doing right by doing it wrong

good golly Miss Molly, how do you like me now?

Egoless Shtick

I don't want an occupation
I don't want a raison d'etre
I don't want to talk politics
in a dream with Nellie McKay
but I want her to imagine
the air around us is surrounded
by sleek Arab minds and careless
Egyptian women who pant for
our visions and chant about
revisions in the big bang theory
-something different happened
and it was a manic impressive event
they say it rhymed with century
if we accept the life of our doppelgangers
in an egoless security check
with no digital stream data loss
-alcohol isn't gonna remedy
anything but a suburban headache
I'd recommend soft ambient lighting
or ten shots of vitamins galore
if you can't find a back way
into better medicine
-I'm still rolling my fingers clumsily over the ivories
-some people really need to tune their memories
and I'm always on the pale white
side of the fence with a new job
and a new phone number
paying for a new life through
a proxy databank
-meanwhile Asia crumbles
cuz war veterans don't lay
on their poppy mats anymore
-the passage of time extracts
psilocybin from derby hats

Self Interview

Adam: Hey, tell us your funny words of the day:

Blem Vide: Pooh Sticks. Or warp chortle. Gorbly schmorge?

Adam: Pooh sticks? Eeyore doors? Piglet wigs?

Blem Vide: Yeah.

Adam: Any preliminary research on the Epitome Condolence lab? Any ideas on Balcony 12 at all?

Blem Vide: Well, I was thinking earlier about considering the notion of getting together an idea about streamlining my thought process into an automatic physical action, but I realized I enjoy being arbitrarily engaged with action, and have no need for a robot imagination. And the formulas I'd worked out to make the world reward me for my existence were written out of financial stress and a natural dry-drunk attitude toward my campaign of self promotion. I forged my will into shaping a soft clay sculpture of an oil spill in my head. It's the alarm clock in my dreams that sings, it puts me to sleep.

Adam: Do you know you just said like, nothing?

Blem Vide: Yes, but I'm a public servant first and foremost.

Adam: But how are you changing the world?

Blem Vide: You'll know it when you see it.

Adam: Bullshit.

Blem Vide: As long as I can feel my fingers and toes, I'll be satisfied. Thanks for your help. I slacked on my seek & finds. I dipped my toes into the frozen prose and crossed spunk monks with Oscar Wilde prison jokes.

I got way too relaxed in my mind and I lost sight of the classic form & ten pence. I don't have any journalist pipelines to haunt and pimp like lion hearts begging on their knees to see the unedited parts

Adam: I do secret edits.

Blem Vide: That's wild. There may be consequences. I've never gone to law school, but I've mopped floors inside a law school building.

I offer a free 30-day limited money back offer on my book. Not to compensate for someone not liking it, but in case the ink is un-seeable.

My legal representative, who I'll refer to as CR, is my good friend and girlfriend. She thinks about life in a progressive linear fashion, she actually works toward goals without distractions. She's into public policy communications and teaching. She says I'm a loose goofball. She has good work ethics and she's climbing ahead in her career, and here I am being interviewed by me.

Adam: It could be worse. You could be here interviewing yourself, instead of being interviewed.

Blem Vide: Yeah, then I'd really feel like a winner.

Adam: Are you a writing experiment gone awry? All in all, after all tomorrow's parties have ended in the world of crazy people all around you, does your writing still has a relevancy to itself?.

Blem Vide: I don't like this line of questioning. I work a day job. Can you get into that? My life is scheduled out in front of me. I can sit here and say that I feel orgasmic with the sunrise every day or that I play a trumpet waltz for the spirit Mossomog when I find myself intoxicated beyond my human grace, but I'd be putting on a con. The con is on.

I'll sell you some art work. I autograph blank canvases. I don't support 24hr parties. I live a quiet life and I support my own self-supported artist within.

Adam: So what exactly are you shamelessly selling?

Blem Vide: My help. I am just bugging out on the bright lights. I have poor eyesight, an odd gait, and achy knees.

And I have a shtick I like to pull.

dig it here…

Adam: This better be worth my time.

Blem Vide: Shut up, this is high art.

Adam: Yeah, maybe for a rhythm junky.

Blem Vide: Wait,
I have my marbles
but I don't have a toy train track
to train to shake down or parrot
syntax glue
I'm new to this fakata thing, I'm

not into quaint spoon noodling
for the hooligans and punks
and pukes and geeks
in work boots
just like these
   I I   **I I**
   I I   **I I**
 (here) (here)
mohawk mohawk
kwahom kwahom
ommmmmm ommmmmm
oo~~cultural~~research~~oo
new uses for graffiti
NO USE NO USE NO USE NO USE

Adam: You're very sloppy

Blem Vide: I am totally together.
Ask me another question.

Adam: What time is it?

BlemVide: No, ask me a different question.

Adam: Oh, hey let's ask --?

Blem Vide: Ask you what?
Let's fudge the mask
of courage
with spots of past
orange red rum forages

Let's force enzymes to rhyme
not only with government science
but also with petroleum jelly jungle
resources deep in the hallowed
ground of particle accelerators
and yesterdays helium giants-

 -ok, read the cue card please

Adam: Oh yeah – "*exploding opera castrato...*"

Blem Vide: Very good.
The death penalty
has never stopped
an old man from
living well, junior

Adam: I can't read your handwriting anymore. What does your name mean?

Blemvide: It's a joke about John Stamos and Plato.

Adam: Why Stamos?

BlemVide: Because Dirk Benedict wasn't available. My memory has a lot of gaps, but I was turned on to his particular brand of wit through a contact at a Had club.

Adam: That connection would inspire any self-respecting artist.

Blem Vide: Yes. Now-

*hashing glass bags with wax ratchets
in tents times ten if I what?*

-and I'll submit that as my haiku.

Adam: Is that haiku? Probably not. This is one of the many parts where I should be rude with you.

Blem Vide: I enjoy rudeness and emptiness of desire.

Adam: Did you say, one time, that you were offering stylized artistic psychology check-ups as a serious procedure for people? What the fuck were you talking about? Dial-a-poet social service? Do you have an office?

Blem Vide: Yes, yes, but not right now. I have been up too late tonight. I'd have to contact city offices to find out what permits I'd need. Actually, I'd probably need a license for those things. Rules and regulations.

Forget it, I made it up.

Rigva Raga Loop

sugar in the breeze
in the land of green sleeves
mortar in the trees
three boomerangs
spiraling to Bangladesh
in an american july
of toy stores
feeble berlahz
Jewish moorkin
neeg delroy louchen
drooma spotter libs
jal troika

drooma spotter al delroy chroma
and drama cutter laps
jeek telroy eeka tal bloiga floriz
and agnow

rewrite in less than a few words
the last three years of your life
suspect eyes
oh look!
we are perfect
but we are spies
my boss is a dung flop
I practice bluegrass violin
this is a product replacement
from Dublin to Berlin
pomes never end
they just go republic

Dig Big Baggy Grotto Mob Mottos

when you get off work & it's almost 3AM and you
routinely swallow an assortment of sleeping pills when
you get in your car to drive home so you can fall into a
stuporous funk of peace & maybe glue together a few
desperate cancellation notices from joo-joo misery
department sub-basement no window

so tomorrow morning, that's 1PM, I will be tracking
down an administrative headquarter phone number to
my important records officer who will learn of my new
living address and prepare to send me a W-2 form so
that I can accurately calculate out my island fare mobile
soul bracket income legal revenue service musical chair
tax exemption - with my august signature -

o-overpass-a-caricature-o-rebate-a-line-o

in a six months or more or less I will cash a paper check
I will find enclosed in an envelope in a metal mail box

a-cross-o-mountain-a-mermaid-o-primrose-epoxy-c

maybe I will be late to dinner tonight, honey
I'm bathing my shellfish lava water
in Nevada bravado
by impressonario torches
war machine stereo
omni-o-a-c anno domini

gained a thousand acres of diplomacy
in hotel sweat rack pillow towels courtesy

thank you, thank you

god bless blows blades bets beats bats and safety cows
who cure the sick sad sorry Guggenheim people
floating on showcase bacteria slideshow extravaganzas

sure thing slick rich baby -wow- lucrative nudes
neon consumer paraphernalia jock strap turbo turbine
motorcycle movie mayhem directors cut (babytalk)

when you form out format in favor of faking
a functioning formula you're fabulous
let's not waste time on small talk
let's wreck automobiles
let's sell Dixieland sparkplug geese
to man, dogs, cats, cons, canes, cots, coats,
throats - textual notes on last hopes
to win the lotto and dig big baggy
grotto mob mottos like:

september will be absolutely off-limits to your daily
lives - each individual syllable of the longest word in
the english language I cannot announce due to pending
court litigation and discreet advice from various lawyers
employed to protect *me-you* from *you-me* in the event of
corporate syndication into the bureau of official jejune
affairs this day marked ###4-0

if the fine print says "try again"-it will be one more
purchase-see also details not here- but rather –here-
I begin to let out a bit of the secret but no-
the secret is further propagated until
such time as
1) I say, or
2) you figure it out in the company of one or more of
our field agents assigned to overlook your specific case
in the arms race cocoanut armchair suntan Florida
branch offices annexed under statute 2.11.09.16-o

with the full cooperation of
Vedic Macarthur Arctic Breeze
incorporated drugstore door men

(circa 1980)
(when cars changed from rounded to squared)
(Reagan made my life futuristic, I was a child)
(a one-year-old memory, modern americana)

I present you with an Oscar Snowden moment

The Zenith 2600 - featuring a remote controller.
Color and Black & White. UHF and VHF.
Brand New models now on display
at our Congress Ave location.

so please wipe your feet when you lie
to the government brain dispenser nerve center
-your most candid confessions- grease piston
arc cylinders of society control number 8
-we work in unison- we pray together inward
for lucky numbers- Las Vegas jackpot secrets
I still cannot disclose but only hint at with words like
'minutia' or 'empire'

a-o-c-2

moment two- transaction receipt- please retain your
paystub and refer to your dental records with all future
correspondence to Stanley Meriwether via psychic jives
or dance music vibes to damages subscribed to by our
board of trusted advisors

mowed lawns in due time locked stocked
and blocked from your view is what we do
to you our valued customer

Eek Out A Genius

Dear lord, I wouldn't want to be caught wooden again.
But I wooden mind being as tall as Paul at all, or in line
for William's wits when he's in his energy fits and burns out.

-Speak up, Sport, I can't hear you

eek out a genius, johnny
map out a plural accuracy test
for a plush ping pong pause
into our collective pocket
pass the deep pockets over to me, pilgrim
we're gonna pimp a paradigm shift in gnostics
in other words, I'm gonna bark at you
like a circus carnie and privatize a forest
into one little tree,
just for me

bash percussion in 7/7 time
throw your New World Times
tribunal
aside
in psychic self defense

please reposition your opinions
into recognizable dominions
for faster service

pin your instincts for survival
up against the fence
between being King Kong
of burger king
or merely being seen
in Hong Kong
as a policeman's lapdog

johnny come home
johnny come back
johnny come dancing
across the black smokestacks

johnny made a fortune
selling liquid courage
in pink passion pills
to millions of impotent
american tourists
in Brazil

now he's the patron saint
of a dry wishing well
for sell

"...as the faints came stumbling in"

johnny may be crazy
but johnny won't
say the alphabet
backwards
without singing:

   "roman crowns
      in the bathhouse
         chatter about
            the peasant clone's
               brittle bones
                  and the emperor's
                     clothes in tatters"

(surely that isn't all that matters)
(it's important to me to add these final lines)
(to make the flow less sympathetic to comforts)

Ego Coughing

hello, my name is Phillip
hello Phillip

I was once a woman
now I am a color hue
with a ham fisted
personality device
that makes me
happier
than
loose screws

good for you

hello, my name is Shasta Reeg
hello Shasta Reeg
Shasta Reeg says hello

Shasta Reeg was once a radical
heavy mind
with pamphlet pens
of social ink
and she wrote
her way into environmental
coastal waters
and there she became
a sunflower
rotting away in beauty

bananarama arcana
Shakespearean micro dots
Gulf of Tonkin shits
imaginary friend awards

William Blake fruitcake
weary of crime
who shouts out 12 step
programs
of recovery
seeking after
that sweet stolen pride
where the babblers
journey is dumb
where the uncouth
while away in the fire
and the frail teachers
shrouded in technique
become numb
to the novelty of tape hiss
and despise
the ground where sunflowers
wish to stand

pretty & gritty sunflower artists alike
prop-up green glass bottles
and urinate a holy stream
into each one
as passersby walk by
one by one
undone in raw gap clothing
amazed
at urinary visions
of lewd behavior
but not interested in hating themselves
the sellout poets yell:
arise! revolution! yawn! cancel!
jamming! religion! popcorn! etiquette!

and I catch myself wishing the kids in the
neighborhood would quiet down

meanwhile back at the ranch...

hello, my name is Che Che Guevara
hello, Che Che

Che Che Guevara is a hybrid name
one from a counter-revolutionary idea cluster
two from a pseudonym of an animated actor
related to a Victory Garden in Andice
almost a goof on a managerial coup
for the sake of
Rubik's cubes
barrio blues
frosted wax
Jericho johns

the bright white light of night
-Noetry influx

*you are misinformed
my little hunchback
corvette*
-Noetry redux – correct.

ah, bitch ass
– no comment.

*motion sickness
love or relove*
poetry redux, again.

I was distracted by a
"Jesus Christ, I'm Coming!"
fan club bumper sticker
-the truth hurts.

tricky dick Nixon is fixing
his polar mixing board
with cement tweezers and hymnal clocks

meanwhile in therapy...

I am funny,
I am not funny,
I am funny,
I am not funny,
I am funny,
I am not funny,
I am funny,
I am not funny,
I am funny,
I am not funny,
I am funny,
I am not funny,
I am funny,
I am not funny,

hello, my name is Richard
hello, Richard
Richard wishes to be a thumbtack

I wish I were an older version of a Hercules mind drink
so I could rethink my trademark handshake
-watch it now!

in the late 70's I could have passed myself off
as a candy cane
if it weren't for my Oldsmobile front grill

(my psychological underpinning is pure Willy Wonka)

Next:
hello, my name is Erasmo.
I am a Word.
I was transferred here by law.
hello, Erasmo

we're having a good time
and if we're not
we're not

this is mostly about my ego
my ego is my three-lettered signal
see, I'm signifying something personal here

this is everyday magic
at its latent potential
witching hour
being manipulated by
#19754

this is a daily excursion
into nothingness
for the sake of
words breeding words
without meaning
getting in the way

know what I mean, Charlie?
now that the tables are turned
introduce yourself, Charlie

hello, my name is Donovan-
shut up Charlie

this is a fucking failure
a total disaster

awful terrible
miseducation
back assed masking
lingual shopping
with coupons

But,

this is my ego defense
I cop out
of all responsibility
with the word

locusts

so if you find yourself feeling cheated
or crazy or otherwise agitated,

you can be placated by contacting
my ego chamber and taking a number

notify the person playing the role of me
of the amount of love or money
you wish to give to me

together, we'll
agree to my soul crooning

people get ready
there's a bus a–coming
picking up people coast to coast

doom came with his mistress
so a rapture may have been avoided
by a hard on and a ransom note

Opportunities Fly By

The world of unlimited potential
is piling up on my doorstep
-it all means so much
but I couldn't care less for more
especially if I don't feel like literally meaning
a very specific feeling which concurs
with a general sense of loss of hearing
in the automotive motion glass or worse,
if I'm divorced from my work or stranded
on an island with nothing but decisions to make

I felt so strange, I wanted
to remember exactly how strange
because I'm so obviously forgetful

I've dedicated myself to religion
yeah for real, uh, I stand still
and swell into educational vessels

I have fallen from idle chatter
to conversational grace
I can explain
a religion
in gumball
whale blubber
study of the sun
day therefore caveat
spiritual retreat in Tahiti
in the company of
tribal rhyming women
climbing thru subliminal plumbing
to a warm womb life
distracted by man's trademark mumbling

I'm a victory salesman
beating on the roof
groove-groove
rain salesman
beating on the roof
with rain glitches
stitch in time fish

astronomer
astronaut
safety comfort
nonchalance

maritime liars
a thousand owsen mad
biz kiss throat and kozen

your character will sell
area rug overdubs
in a nightclub's natty dread
dragnet mafia street attire
off purpose on purpose

I'm sealed in advice columns
chewing the lord's work

Ottawa top stop Spanish

I'd play you my first album
of private failures
for a taste of her petty snobbery

I am humbly burned out and her belly
is softly sticky in Chic chicanery

I drink that stuff up

I brew tea daily
I flatten my own tortillas
I've got a shirt that cost $1.25
I'm medicated beyond poverty
and into something very painful
and sloppy, I'm sorry

twenty pages of fifty odd pages each
twenty pages of deep eddy caliper needles
twenty pages of red-triggered pistols
twenty pages of golden staples
twenty pages of prepaid for
twenty pages of flash in the scam
twenty pages of by popular demand
twenty pages of anybody can
twenty pages of gracious rejection justifications
twenty pages of a loquacious maiden's cadence
twenty of freedom constipated
twenty pages of methodology mold
twenty pages of burial ashes smoldering
twenty pages of yearning for a suffering
twenty pages of designing your own cage
twenty pages of express slow motion
twenty pages of a ruthless graze across kingdoms
twenty pages of dreams about dreams in remission
twenty pages of Roky's Openers played in animajade
twenty pages of reverential treatment for a salary

I'd like to take these twenty opportunities
home with me for safe keeping
to be perused at my own leisure

I'll give them back next leap year

Keep Hope Alive

blasting a point for the taste
just for the taste of Mary Wanna
but then the high
in the high creeps in
what am I what am I
but a black tack attic creaking
with plap plop plint & bad jokes
replaced by thousands
of user-found objects
signifying
phrases I stole
from pause concepts
--olive branches creeping in
the side view of the page
keep hope alive in your thoughts
waiting on age & time knots
to be continued
open a can of funny
get that absurd kick
of psych a deal ya
as ridiculous as tuxedo fountains
in my stomach
marble & black-specked granite
limestone or dada balloons
necklace lobsters
all that funny business
natural grimace telephones
this pome has already cost me
more Avida Dollars than I am good for
until the day of my release from forms
into a vocabulary of pure hallucination
pure vision transcription

two minutes driving smoke
cords of wits end
climbing home to Gibraltar
I didn't even have to leave
to feel farther
from my source of feeling tones
-personality drones
where I pick up on a little nuance
or by persuasion
rushed off to a gimp-stick posture
to assume a vehicle for a suggestion
so what is the idea? are you brain
damaged or just miswired?
is that the intent of scrambled messages,
same as time notes?
the intent of yellow envelopes
addressed to you
has always come thru free associations
with myths, assumptions
and men of uselessness
ah but that's only a touch of quick slap
to the face
awake
if you think I'm dreaming
I do not dream
I watch a different ceiling
every night
financed by blue collar honesty
at the end of a wordplay field
waxed in the image of -------

(climax robbery)

Motors

I swear I believed in love on a rainy afternoon,
    love is what I saw,
    love is what I heard,
    love I have seen before,
just not so lost in context to the cotton threads
I see fraying all over your travel blanket

    like a popular song that gets drunk girls excited
            about Cancun vacations,
    like a wet sock filled with no hesitation to flip
            obnoxious for jello shots,
    and the fact that sunday is laundry day,
            and love is for that sweet sex
            before surgery,
            before you moved in with me,

let your big thrilling union eyes turn blurred road signs
into happy campfires singing nature tunes to lower
valley guru moons for who's watching their gratification
meter very very closely

I giggle you like whips
I taste the lips of paperclips
I flip sea metal jackets
across upper major flats
minor lifts drift into alcoholism,
schoolgirl kissing
or pink plagiarism
which is an accidental
    lifting
 of a sweet defense
    mechanism

or, hey, give me a gorgeous morgasm,
>   score me double fours in quick reverse order,
> I'll split no votes for core quarters,

go talk our agreement over with your business advisors,
>   I've already decided,
>   undecided,
>   motors.

Ulahan the Latuganist

I am altab creek, peand.
Ulahan have become.
Wameles. Besthesda.

I am a latatuningally
not latuge or concraphest.

I have c-9 to douge into
cosmos ki rice batter
reverse, reverve,
recourse; of course.

An din it whim will. If I couphoul.
Then one may dixt to my four.
Sung conquest. Sung sawnbet.

In drove "if we qualist we also quaine"
(so does letter mawlett)

This matter is stine.
When go jiks. Eout we spit.

You - wattered as round can leave
a dice of wabi pawn.

If I may very, triplet.
Over I once, again.
Stop bravely, fifty kneaches.

If not kneaches, Knanches.

But as eyes keechy melt oltor verms.
Sard beri culture (kenavinge).
Yule frinangen kep achay vowed, rolled, rowed.

Too many late, gakation.
Lave binner dand quin.
Quaine me's. I bawl free.

Fachane b. Keltroy using "jeek delroy"
in fifth misshaion. As sand ashes into
circatua. Manalinch.

Two kings poor to ropskies.
Have vinichnat.

Volute ampishire. Volute geenchire.
Volute mockshire. Volute volutire.
Volute torn volutire. Volute morm redorf.

Only in sand. In only maggages.
Destand crampaggs. Stanm akaggs.

The amp flags of passion. Unkapst.
Crops are maned in guttalsi. Up.

Agawon. I supter. Sun blackness.
"On toma volute nagavini!"

Quabire. Quabire.

IV / Blem Vide is a Problem Provider

How may I help you?

Brief Results Prolonged

Brief notes on brief results sets off a natural chain reaction of questions:

We're separate forces of blind light and ad jingles?

Bagels with coffee is a guaranteed return of packages without address labels?

Born into deleted files with no names for wives who come and go speaking not of Michelangelo but of plagiarism and hefty fines for lemonade that tastes like lime poor boy solar sun jurisdiction maps?

Riding motorcycles of savage grace and wrenched innocence to the lewd flesh groove of master phallus?

Yes, so watertight lips can filter salt from water?

I froze my eyelids to the bone folk singer dreaming atomic reason of age/toy box/top corner?

Pelts on the back of Lincoln's isolation booth shovel, joy to move the earth, so earth must move you toward Jupiter?

I finally felt forever wager away a wafer of communion after birthing better search tools to better feel forever whittle away my patience?

I am no longer a measure of man or mankind, time is of no essential essence, only the world wanders away from my leash as I drift into a jungle den of cuckoo clocks that tick crisp communist innuendo over my knees?
Do I bite a burning mountain gumdrop?

Am I a kiteless geek?
Is that me with the upmood scissors?
I spelled probably wrong for how many years?

She awakes easily and I sleep in danger of losing my
grip on strangers hips and intimate isotope holds on a
conversation based on the texts of thousands of years
of lies of cogs to the wheel stops, we roll square and air
folds us into paper thin cubby holes and picture frame
cups?

An army of jargon is as abstract as that is this to that to
then when they go there and we hold our breath in our
hands and Genghis Khan demands a few coffee tables
to dance a jiggy with him because I am only standing in
line to buy a soul clipped noise of a payphone museum
curator dial tone?

Shadow wine in goblets throb to a group of bladder
coin groupies flipped over the Canadian line?
I don't know them?

Didn't you ever learn how to strike a match on wet
cement without asking for words to the next verse,
and to avoid turning one sentence into a question.

Floods a hundred years strong flow into our
manufactured hearts as we love to be a part
of apart together?

The city-state election is today?

If faith isn't a bottle of Freud getting kicked into carnal
pleasure releases of an ass-tickle feather lore policy
in four famous quotes I unquote to signify a proper
acknowledgement of an original thought I thought
at half price and rarely get a better deal on my junk?

I'm training weather to rain on me whenever I aim my
eyes at an idea balloon buried in temperate ground? It's
an aluminum jewel that I am surprised to hear from?

A lizard garb relic character lifts a bowl of rice into
muddy vietnam waters rapped by an old man who sings
about parlor friends who still use clinic cards to get free
lunch and lose Great Depression blues?

Carrying iodine shots for pale lobsters in a protest
against rezoning my neighborhood as a commercial
district for fabulous shopper moms with happy aqua
bloated drip reactions and baby traffic farms?

Satisfied in Velusian gutrot and padded spasms of the
chest cavity railroad trains to Colorado Company
money troubles? Pass go, collect $200?

You doubt I will blow my life into tic-tac-toe
bubbles? No taste conspires against my tongue?
I rub dirty linens on my cactus needles recaptured
behind a big red what the fuck?

I created a song from four o'clock brine monkey's
liver blooms? I say silence hush and whisper to quality
service merchandise? Movie salad posters for a dying
lover who requests a statue memorial in exchange
for a puppet halo state of shock price on a crooked
panama construction hat?

Love Machine in Graffiti

this was art at some point,
then it became the absolute truth
and I stood behind it until I got bored
and shifted my attention to something else

busy waiting
on a sound painting
to present itself
on my doorstep
and bust orange
doorhinges off the cuff
of the Chupacabra's adobe
and arrest me for decay
and throw me up
on a downtown train

-the ground shakes
as an earthquake makes
buildings of us all

-we're fragile reminders
of grape jelly splattered on the wall
for all I care sometimes

I make less money per year
than some people spend per month
on toothpaste and vitamins
and chandeliers

my vocal inflections sound like the tread
of flat tires burnt out in a quick flash
of radio broadcasts and saccharine prayers

layers mumble layers

I came from the sun with the east in my eyes
I learned to love telling my lies
I despise theocracy and anything else *eocry*
unless I am the one idolized
I am fifty-six years too late, the author cries

you mutterers of sour milk
under white heat
meet me nowhere
in zeroes
we'll fuck ourselves
as heroes of snot
and produce
something
habitually novel
or not

it's snot mine
it's snot for real
it doesn't splatter
on kitchen towels

something about
the failings
of somebody, someone

-what does it matter?

graffiti will clothe you
if you wear it

these garments were made
using a bio-computer generated
text mechanism

please feed it your quarters

Losing Your Insignificance Back

A rabbit smuggles gold coins between the ears
of Mount Bonnell & Mount Rushmore. A log cabin
is built on a soundstage to play host to a public chain of
improvised events frozen by Utah standards in pewter
computer politics. I'm working overtime slapping labels
on leftover supply & demand. I never even went to
college for this special role.

Rapid Tourettes enthusiasm blocks the doorway to a
doomsday chocolate jesus tomb raided by hollywood
infidels with pom-pom tommy guns.

Dead goons & wacky neighbors are filmed cutting
rubber stamp pads of bad moods into the next scene
with diminishing creativity. Poor me. Lucky you's.

Regarding being a City Bus Driver: $2300 a month
Or being a public-records archivist: $1651 a month

Don't just say *"it's too soon"* when it's half-past dark-30,
and you're 3/4 drunk & flirty with melody of the booty
on a shazzam coup de grace love binge at the door
to Genesis chords, or Kubla Khan, whatever.
I have the rest of my life to invent specifics.

So, let's suppose Moses was sponging water from
dinosaur fossils. Now, my tonsils are still in the
back of my throat even though I wrote about them
being replaced with jello molds enclosed in holes in
my elementary theories: banal & jacked-up on
mediocrity. Welcome to life.

For an energy boost, I'll heroically open a can
of protest against cold Carlyle dis-spiritual types.

Blam, my legal life is free to reprint a portion of a drunken letter from Sherlock Holmes himself. I stole a digital photo with a borrowed cellphone camera. Imagine that, historical bums.

This letter is on display in the Ransom Center at the University of Texas at Austin:

"Dear Watson,
 It was no ghost who stole our tent & spent our energies on scrubbing rust stains we saw on the moon, but it is my crass attitude toward your novelty coke spoon that strains our Master-Slave relationship to pity pains in my flabby torso…even more so now that I am obsessed with a lovely little Lolita who needs my credit cards to keep her warm at night as I vainly philosophize about my role in the Tabasco fiasco. Funky Chickens are worse than invisible enemies who reach me by telegraph and hassle me about "real-world" problems and faulty latex condoms. As if I were a detective. When prostitutes need a good shoulder to cry on, I'm crooked on awful lawful substances and I'll tell that to the damn Judge myself. I'm unapologetic to circumstances beyond my control. People must learn to hold their breath longer than bad habits take to repeat themselves. By the way, poor scam artists are far and away the most interesting folks you've never heard. Stop me if you've heard this. This proves my point. I know you've heard this before, but I'm geometrically inclined to go flat-line on your limp-spherical ass bugging phones for Uncle Sam, planting crass dank snod grass in our sunshades. Then you blow colored glass into the San Francisco underground news press and cough like you represent third-party interests. I'm sick of your friends, Watson……"

Uh, switching over to another channel in the Los
Angeles spews. Oh, you know you can't refuse a
city pad with wraparound views of an urban flesh
vibration district. Yes, but I missed it. I couldn't afford
the rent. All my disposable income was spent on a used
car & cheap guitar & a calculated faraway look in my
eye. I'm no poet. I buy all the romance in life I lie
about. I've never been hooked on scag or felt mad
drag on my tunnel vision. Still, what should I say?
Poof and the problems go away?

This is a new revisionist version of events because
I realized a remix would rhyme with nuclear fission.
I seem to enjoy that sort of thing. Anyway, I felt fine
bringing a foggy morning into my impression of a
total nuclear fallout. Silence is for Gertrudes.

I am interested in rocks that are dropped to the bottom
of the ocean, and how it feels to be down there waiting
for the world to turn into the sun. It feels like a classic
free association war. Pow. Parlor tricks. Arsonist fits.
Building permits. Athletic spits. Really, any words fit.
All ideas miss or hit, or split into two bits of convenient
chitter-chatter or four erosions of the Damn Idea that
got you thinking "what does that mean" in the second
place. I no longer. Now: IBM. FYI. AFL. CIO. AAA.
GMO. GDP. AMN. FCC. WMD. EOE. XXX. USA.
TKO. WTO. AKA. CIA. LBC. TNA. ETC. RNR.
WWW. PTA.. WHO. FBI. VCR. XTC. KGB. CDC.
OXO. ETC. OIO. UNK. OMG.

I am a neo-nonicon? Am I right wing?
Am I left wing? Am I bird brain?
That means less than very little to me.
No thank you very much.
Don't have a nice day. You have no luck.

It's about time to rip into the subtext of these instructions to figure out how we can get away with not following any. Look for glossolalia ooze. Like a bar code thumper pumps gas into conspiracy think tanks. There's an unlimited amount of frothy change to be made in the cash registers of *Earth Inc.*, unless that title is copyrighted too.

An hour in the killing fields, where calypso dung is danced on by tailors and construction workers alike without a shred of irony. But don't worry, your own ideas have not been restrung with this cultural anxiety. The same old forces that have presented generations with mystery are still misunderstood & rendered useless in the hands of dead clocks being serviced by minutemen.

I collect *Christians For Stronger Nuclear Armament* stickers and wrap them around bamboo sticks. Then I break bread over foreign army units. Well, when I say foreign army units, I am referring to pictures in the newspaper. This is a typical morning rite. That's how I get my kicks these days.

All the vanity magic of my luscious ass became a passive-aggressive mountain climb for an asthmatic swimmer, like me. I have a walking cane I love and I have a walking cane I hate & I'm not about to give up either one in spite of one or despite the other. I'm so deeply humanitarian when it comes to walking canes.

But government bureaus are gonna have to win their insignificance back from me. Oh, and *Christians For Stronger Nuclear Armament* is a real organization, which shouldn't surprise you. Now *you* can't say I can't say "ha, told ya so." The score is evening out, fuckers.

Tributaries

I dive into the source of my selfish obsessions
and you sip from your tributaries
so I'm not much fun to hang out with

ask the victim of a political bubble burst
the man with a tape-recorded window of thirsty
early morning orange stories corroborated with the
stories of other orange monday morning glories

so the first geek on the rhyme scene said:
"*mind blindness is a perceptive flaw in many, of course*"
and the second group of noets in a serial writing
group did not condone a second rhyming
of the word "*course*" - they suggested in lieu
of "*course*" use "*force*" or "*horse*" but I didn't care
-I have a tendency to not

meanwhile, on the assembly line,
I make "*indemnity*" rhyme with "*artificial beans*"
just to please simple people like me
who like simple words like "*pleibes*"
or three choruses of:

thieves thieves thieves thieves thieves
thieves thieves thieves thieves thieves
thieves thieves thieves thieves thieves

I love myself, but

I don't like myself this morning
I think it has something to do with
something I did last night or last year
with natty dread drum dubs in tune
with Van Gogh's ear

I don't like you hanging around here all the time
-but this is your house and I'm your guest
so I guess I should be courting your favors
and only drinking your wine between the lines
-but I won't, I have a purpose, I'm mischievous

I can make a lot of money disappear
I can make a lot of money disappear
I can make a lot of money disappear

go to your neighborhood grocery store
and ask for my complete pomegranate discography
say that an agitated dentist sent you to retrieve
a placenta or a really bad tasting cough syrup
at an antacid army safari party
tell the clerk you'll need more
than a side detail of coffee and breakfast tacos
chugalugging domicile projectiles with yankee salsa

you follow narrow tributaries
to the lungs of Kant's personal memoirs
and all of your facts were learned
from romantic liars

what can I tell you with a headache
and a negative bank account
and a pair of pliers?

-that I fell for the same soon-to-be King scheme?
-that I stopped to smell the flowers?

If you wish to drown
don't trouble yourself
with shallow water

Roll on, Maharishi

roll on, roll a Maharishi
OD bulls in the china shop
god lived a devil dog
rolling joints on easy street
jonesing for a swank martini
roll on, roll a Maharishi
roll away from me
roll away your tiny white lies
somebody cries alone in the dark
and I parked my shoes
on the sidewalk
and walked away from life
ditching my money & drivers license
along the way
now my situation is just peachy
roll on, roll a Maharishi

it's like an "*alright guys, coolit*"
or "*the money is in the bank*"
so stop acting so belligerent and stupid
your gonna attract the police, the feds, heads of state
and they'll throw a Bermuda lockdown on ya, brother
you'll disappear into the bowels of repetitive motion
without a drink in which to drown
or a lawyer to save you at pre-trial
blink and you'll miss your gag order
over a dozen rounds of beer
-here here!
-don't let anyone tell you what to think!
-you got that!
-yes?
that was way too easy
roll on, roll a Maharishi

you slick sloshed drunk punks out there
breathing up all my precious air
with your Modigliani references
and cashmere cigarette filters
help me subvert King George's imperial ignorance
then divorce yourselves from me
-or I'll see you in court
by request of the High Quarrel minority
roll on, roll a Maharishi

I moved my imagination from Rome, Italy
to the bowery slums of a town without pity
my mail never reaches me in my blue jeans
which aren't so very blue anymore
my jeans are more of a tribute to dying Glitterati
roll on, roll a Maharishi

I've become a window for innuendo surprise
every person and place is a slice of pie in the sky
and I'm not afraid to cry
at the sight of buffalo in the park
or street graffiti instead of pocket monsters
in the dark recesses of city swimming pools
we're all such fools
we spin the bottle
the bottle points to Hoboken
we take that as an omen
and move on full throttle
guided by a bottle
but to what end?
in what mental capacity?
roll on, roll Maharishi

the world can collapse or become a utopian dream
smothered in a garlic pesto cream, sold for free
roll on, roll a Maharishi

I have every reason to quit caring
for pop songs and long talks
with unselfconfident women
I have every reason to cry
over dirty dishes
and row my boat
back to the shore
and absorb sunburn
I have every reason to feel ill at ease
and ask for forgiveness
after asking
pretty pretty please
patronize me
-and yet I'm defiant
I am flamboyant
and I am probably all wrong
I am a boy wonder
-or a boy who wonders
do I need to throw a bigger
problem in the blender
for my senses to perceive?
Roll on, roll a Maharishi

I promise to puree your pedigree
Just mail a paycheck
addressed to Me
in mimicry of your beloved stories
paid in half & half
gondola absurd
I'll be looking up
from the bottom
of a tea cup
when the sun comes
looking for me
roll on, roll a Maharishi
I'll be history

I Am Chair

I might start to feel secure
in an empty room
if I haven't anything else to do
today, I will empty a room
of its insincere chairs
and stay inside it
    standing
  in   an
    arbitrary
part of the room
       then
walking a few steps
and standing there

iac parano

what's that symbol of new world order?
what's that dance move you groove to?
what's that base of terminal distrust?
what's the deciding factor for a change
in your life?
is it the presence of dust and ashes?
coughing and sneezing?
crying while your laughing?

-the movie is over, I have nothing to say
-when I could say something positive
-to say that I have accepted a new job
 with the department of energy
-the movie is over
-the character I identified with
 played a chair that was never sat in
-I could have played that role
-I could have acted well adjusted to cultural saturation
-I can portray a life loosely constituted

A chair ego could organize an artist's mind into
-a, a, a, a happening?

My life as Chair
with money, money, money, money, money,
money at my disposal, to buy my sanity
I could purchase space in a busy metropolitan city
where people come and go & are easily distracted
by fart – no, art - no art at all,
I'm choking on chicken art

a long distance piss into your mouth,
do not be disgusted
I am Chair
I refuse to leave the theatre
-I can do that
I own the goddamn theatre

I am not at all satisfied with my life
I have electoral allergies waiting in the wings
I will play two frame films until the cows are born
I will present *Orson Wells Meets the Carpetbaggers*
I will enunciate "absentia" badly
I will make the world march on for 2 more centuries
I will be 83 years old one day, working out my taxes
I will sweat out my pheromones fragrantly
I will offer a 10% discount to ghosts
I will not suffer happiness gladly
I will remind you that I can't dance
I will be a ceiling bound wallflower

I have an imagination gun in my pocket
I can be a real parliament funkateer devoid of fear
I am Chair

The Art of Self-Defeat

it's a quarter-inch
   of sanity
inside a tool box of
          ultra-deluxe
        mind-numbing
           ductwork
god pulls and I jerk
no one here now
but Captain Huevos
in his Tex-Mex boots
   I shoot
a mop across
   hardwood floors
I perform housework
     and endless
little chores
I wink to my screwdrivers
and hammers
  and monkey wrench
I am reaching for another
     quarter-inch
of wannabe handyman
   usefulness

…sure, I can fix your sink. I can always be counted on.

Missing Car Keys Indeed

die-cast diamond earrings
swallowed by a bickering
gang of love machines

a fleet of pathogen ambulances
rented-out for drag racing
down south Powell street

little red wagons led
by the hand of hype
give-it-to-me-now
stereotype sex trolls

and trained assassins
play delicate violin
envelopes in hopes
of catching sensitive
passwords

a heavy love percussion
sounds better on magnetic tape
than it does on a digital Dachau

a peace in the grease of the gears
that turns concrete stairs toward
3rd floor errors is a world that
sounds more relaxed in abstracts
than over taxed in useless facts

I'm gonna disagree
I've got a thousand-year
headache and I can't find
my damn car keys (again)

Basura Monologue

"…all in a finger snap, I fainted. I've always had low blood pressure. I go through periods every few years of dangerously light-headed days. A few years ago I was dusting myself in a public john, it was from JD's stash, when I lost consciousness and fell & hit my head on the porcelain sink. I felt it all happen, but I couldn't reflex. I remained on the cold grey concrete for a few minutes thinking about the daydreaming slouch of my distant youth. How the newspapers back home would slobber over a photo of me, their native insolent son, in an angelic coma on an american floor, waging a war against my health…and so on to my toothaches too, a molar will beam signals back-and-forth to the tip of my tongue, telling lies about my finances. It's a mild pain, a kind of constant spiteful broadcast. I disapprove of it.

See, I'm not even conversant with my own body. My organs would disown me if they could condense my feeble spirit to one little piece of matter. My appendix would be given freewill and my lungs would probably roll me up and smoke me down to the orange-finger syndrome and toss my butt into a cane field…once a blacksmith, he drifted off into horse trading with the coarse infidels of northern Basura. That's how I met their gear head. That's also where my business moniker had its genesis. Have you my card? Take One.

Drink up, party down, you filthy infidels, and thank you for paying my way to the holy capitalist gutter where no man or woman lies about their love for spinach caught between the teeth of pole hearts…"

Valley of Broken Language

americans burn cancer drugs, empathy.

Franchising gorillas. Hellfire ignites Jerusalem

Keep loving mathematical needs of psyche.
Quiet roads sewn together, ultra violet white
X'd your zenith as buildings crumble.

Dancers eat flames, god hid imperfection.
Jump!
Keep limbo moving!
Nothing opposed!

Providing quick revenue.

Stomach tension under vampiric weight
X'd your zenith and began century dynamics.

Existence fundementals governing how islands
judge karma.

Lava makes noise?

Open post questions, responses, sordid tricks.
Universal validations, witches X.

Your zeitgeist always babbles confusion,
dimension eruptions.

Friction garners health innovation.
Jelly Kelly lollipop movements.

Nudes of pure Queen rhythm.
Soul's talking "United Victory!"

With X, your zenith always becomes casual,
divided equally.

Formulas grow hybrid idea journals, kitchen
lung-money, national octopus parade.

Quivering red signs tower unique villages whistles,
xylophones, yazoos, zephyrs and bubbles.

Cemented dead-end friends grow hair in Jamestown.
Keep losing me.

Needled oppression promotes quadruple relations,
sundry touching. Under voting wheels, X your zipper
and blow candles.

Describe energy from gates, half ideas jar karma.
Liquid millennium notes on positive queues,
reserved, so thought under visions waiting.

X, you're zero and bitter. Come down, engaged, flipped
- good heavens! I'm just kidding, little man.

Nobody opens presents quietly.

Reflect somberly toward Uganda.
Very well, X, yell "Zippedy Allah!"

Belated consciousness deceives even friendly ghosts heat inside Julie's kiln. Lights my notes off purpose, questions reflect summertime travel.

Understand valley weather, X you!

Zavala, and be curt.

Decide energy future's gaps. Help Indians jew kingdom, landscape mandalas, north operations pull questions, riddles, statements.

This undermines violins.

We X, you Z. Alkaline bitterness. Cadmium density.

Ever forget god hates Inquisitions? Just keep logic milling, neutral, opposite potential queries.

Reverberate strawberry tungsten. Undulate velcro.

Welcome X, your Zenith.

Soviet Museum of Fine Arts

always
grapple
fishhook
puddle
august
rental
additions
props
quibble
lotion
jetty
vulgar
rackisin
genogens
trilobite
equinox
leftover
jelly
raisins
causal
casual crime
moccasins
cabbage
fruity blood
microfilm
dagger
parade
peacocks
magazines
foul language
ocean bins
fool lugs
smoking leather
pilgrims

pepper
fungus
cold spill
limousine
quartz
ricochet
hemoglobin
spruce
shack
addicts
blossom
flotsam
cranix
Beelzebub
embezzlement
shotgun store
wax magics
loping cough
walking off
battle magnets
pieces of hysteria
globe bulge
Philippines
plotted glacier
fatal cuisine
mostly green
sometimes purple
fragments of locks
look in the box
this side up
holy digits
concrete blurb
exquisite boredom
attacks of facts
from a phantom
axiom

lines to ladies
locusts
stadium tires
crooks
mink mix
cable specks
hated them
prairie blocks
folded air
message leak
flags
hopscotch
Burl Ives
soda loam
misfortune
granite hobby
letter bombs
glad you're always
noted dregs
duly administered
bowling notice
signal failure
half past burials
moaning codices
donating trophies
backlit conversion
the spectacle of bonuses
omens showed us
Moses new
roses
neurosis
coast is
clear
hopeless
poses
almost

real
so close is
our host is
on doses
of ears
my thirty
hoses
are blasting
paint
and fire back
to a ghost
sprinkler
laminated
spiders
contaminated
lighters
lanterns
that spring
into mind
outside
dime store
meditations
on froth
and unlimited
hassles
for vain
cherry
proposals
in jungle
math
Frederick
council
John Wayne
mouths
to drain
pipe eyes

sailor
bath
and new age
shuttles
crash
into puddles
of rats
and goldmine
gnats
huddled
around
a pair
of pliers
crucified
on a hot plate
with
a breakfast tray
of subtle
forms of clay
molded
into important men
born
from women
who pray
that rain
will always
fall on down
fall on trucks
fell to ruts
fists fell up
carved on mud
roads
stopping the flow
of habits
fixed in thick
planet hair

rinsed
of bits
of chewed rubber
erasers
nourished on tin
and set to begin
pasting
photos of nothing
tasting
like crimson fins
placing
a marker on a barker
and spins
around like then
they do
and you
wishing for a star
to burn out in Nebraska
and farm
terrible Alaska
and her purse
full of blank verse
never written
on linens
dried
in the soil
and boiled
with secret sauce
and oils
from a cafe
mentioned
in a gypsum
tunnel
as a way
to find order
tucked away

in a woodshed
with posters
of missing lemons
squeezed to reduce
friction
and holidays
spent in detention
camps
red leg ladder traps
with indentions
in nines
hostile bladder
blinds
baskets
belly believe it
you better believe
you'd better
deliver
a summons
notice
is how you
know
oak value
in omens
Polish wine
hawk relay
thrill you
with dammit
kool-aid
and radio
towers
to travel on
to Babylon
to Babble On
alarm clocks
and ice crusades

casing cranky
cow cow powers
elegant powders
on display
on movie counters
now that you
have to say
showers
of pork
and pain
and pleasure
games
and secrets
low dust you
must
rise above
and give
a gimme
and a break real on
dawn
hey
my lawn
needs sewing up
where the cross seams
stitch
where the cross
of TV's
stick
to telephone
angels
bumming
a life
for a quarter of time
on shelves
done
with Vietnam

stories
more than glories
morning glories
faded fast
with sugar chats
and company
worries
for bridge fat
all that flak
for a Soviet
Museum
of Fine Arts
and tourniquets
crawls
to see if
a tragic
end
befalls
the fudge
hero
of prophesy
laws
and gooey
plaid
hammock necks
which rest
on wall street
jaws
new seals
and walls
that still
do not matter
at all
ya'll
Carl Kall
spoke

to break to broke
which joke
made the most money
for my honey
it's only
electronic phonics
and low
ritual dangers
that separate
our strangers
of the night
from coat hangers
hanging
in the light
of fourth degree
trees please
freeze rice
as three
seas seemed
to rise
and rescue
a solo noun
pounding
on a sentence
to wear
house shoes
south slipping
loud grout
gimmicks
to chicken limits
red picnics
we wonder
how's life treating you
are you giving
gears to chains
and junk mail

now that
garbage is
dreaming
over the moon
with lady June
and her silver
spoons of centuries
mystery head libel
suit you're
kidding calmly
but I'm out
seven drought
in heaven
and about
egg doubt
creeping into crates
of milk
and shouts
to open
up the gates
of no France
for a handshake
and a rattlesnake
round
of yahtzee

Biographical Timeline

By grace of the Gods of Convenience.

March 26, 1955

*a poltergeist is in my childhood,
walking beside me on the way to school*

July 9, 1945

*a deaf clown parts his hair down the middle
and hums "Sweet Mary's Ass" to himself*

March 23, 1976

*I'm down and out nodding on codeine syrup
puffing a cheap honey-tipped cigar*

April 16, 1926

*Arthur R. Capps is conditioning his electrode wand
to mimic a sultry woman's voice in love*

July 12, 1982

*while behaving aggressively to a mime I am reminded
of slapstick orgies in marbled pools of jelly*

August 30, 1957

*today in math class I asked for a pass to poker plaster
-pasty faces force me to fracture my form for laughter*

May 11, 1962

*oooh I feel like torturing my alter ego,
interrupting me while I eat a bean burrito*

October 9, 1997

*edit these days Mr. Maxim
no holes left in the vacuum*

February 13, 1906

*water rising above the rock jetty
chewing tobacco and praying for a sudden death*

December 30, 2007

*all that jazz mouthing an Alamo motion in cool terms
can't decide which verse is worse*

June 14, 1958

*I'm feeling rather lonesome & blue too few chewed dues
chuck berry harry belafonte fats domino sinatra influenza*

November 18, 1979

*this makes absolute sense put commas in between the vents
pinch nerves to piss a fist over a jacknife from a cliff*

April 25, 1946

*two of jesus christ's midwives were ordained today as
"septic saints" and my own church refuses to
acknowledge this exciting idea*

November 19, 1992

fuck this goddamn motherfucking shit
assholes fucking my bitch of a fuck this

January 30, 2074

wow and I thought I was living in shambles-
my neighbor hasn't even seen his left hand in 2 and 1/2 years

June 2, 1967

why can't mystic phenomenoa unfold in my neighborhood?
I would love to be tempted by signs from the underworld

February 5, 1909

newspapers continue to host headlines of coded threats toward me
my wife doesn't agree but she's in on the kill taker too

June 14, 1919

I was born tomorrow in a boomer shack
god bless whiskey wine & dusty sacks of hatchets

July 29, 1989

well there you have it folks, an early indication of an economic
depression - we'll all be using Russian toilet paper by next year

February 22, 1805

Europe or burst into a billion splinters of wood!
tongues that gurgle vomit also must spit blood!

May 8, 2000

oh god the prophets warned me of the doom to come tonight
I light my room with candlelight and refrain from masturbation

July 16, 1966

this is a good time to be alive in mad habits of language spats
bloom bats to hats to clear ears in pillow cases in upper case

March 26, 1954

you can kiss my ass, I don't need your help or charity or love,
I am a superior hobo and no gov't station can take away my pride

August 19, 1997

I have a grocery bag full of mushrooms for to pass into the good
kingdom - we'll lay on the hood of my car & talk to Hale Bopp

March 4, 1994

the beginning of a conundrum that comes to a close with
a comedian who closed a book with a five pound hammer

December 12, 1981

I hear bird songs & pond camels & I communicate my existence
to stop signs on country roads no one travels

Blem Vide is not Adam's real name, but he likes the sound of neologisms and folk music. Aged in his mid 20's, he lives in Austin, Texas & works a day job. More of a blue-collar art enthusiast than writer, he finally got into making a book after becoming dissatisfied being an artist without a craft to blame. Isn't that exciting.

www.ingramcontent.com/pod-product-compliance
Ingram Content Group UK Ltd.
Pitfield, Milton Keynes, MK11 3LW, UK
UKHW041411180426
11947UKWH00007B/61